A Toolkit of Motivational Skills

A Toolkit of Motivational Skills

Encouraging and Supporting Change in Individuals

Second Edition

Catherine Fuller and Phil Taylor

John Wiley & Sons, Ltd

Copyright © 2008   John Wiley & Sons Ltd, The Atrium, Southern Gate, Chichester,
West Sussex PO19 8SQ, England

Telephone (+44) 1243 779777

Email (for orders and customer service enquiries): cs-books@wiley.co.uk
Visit our Home Page on www.wiley.com

Clip art in psychoeducational materials © 2005 Microsoft

7 2014

Other Wiley Editorial Offices

John Wiley & Sons Inc., 111 River Street, Hoboken, NJ 07030, USA

Jossey-Bass, 989 Market Street, San Francisco, CA 94103-1741, USA

Wiley-VCH Verlag GmbH, Boschstr. 12, D-69469 Weinheim, Germany

John Wiley & Sons Australia Ltd, 42 McDougall Street, Milton, Queensland 4064, Australia

John Wiley & Sons (Asia) Pte Ltd, 2 Clementi Loop #02-01, Jin Xing Distripark, Singapore 129809

John Wiley & Sons Canada Ltd, 6045 Freemont Blvd, Mississauga, ONT, L5R 4J3, Canada

Wiley also publishes its books in a variety of electronic formats. Some content that appears in
print may not be available in electronic books.

Library of Congress Cataloging-in-Publication Data

Fuller, Catherine.
   A toolkit of motivational skills : encouraging and supporting change in individuals / Catherine
Fuller and Phil Taylor. – 2nd ed.
      p. cm.
   Includes bibliographical references and indexes.
   ISBN 978-0-470-51658-4 (pbk. : alk. paper)   1. Motivation (Psychology) 2. Employee
motivation. 3. Motivation (Psychology)–Problems, exercises, etc. 4. Employee motivation–
Problems, exercises, etc. I. Taylor, Phil. II. Title.
   BF503.F85 2008
   153.8'5–dc22

                                                                              2008002741

British Library Cataloguing in Publication Data
A catalogue record for this book is available from the British Library

ISBN 978-0-470-51658-4 (P/B)

Typeset in 13/18 pt New Baskerville

Printed and bound by CPI Group (UK) Ltd, Croydon, CR0 4YY

Contents

About the Authors

Catherine Fuller MA, PGCertEd is a staff developer for the National Probation Service of England and Wales and runs an international training consultancy. She helps practitioners and their managers, in a variety of settings, develop skills, understanding and confidence to facilitate change in others. Her background includes over 20 years as a practitioner, manager and staff developer. Catherine and Phil were at the forefront of developing motivational work with offenders in England and Wales and Catherine has since helped to establish motivational cultures in the new probation services of Turkey, Bulgaria and Romania.

Information about training packages based on this book is available from: Catherine Fuller Associates

---

Catherine Fuller Associates provide tailor-made consultancy and training on Motivational Skills to assist the implementation of the ideas in this Toolkit into practice.

Catherine Fuller Associates can be contacted at:

Cop Castle
Bringsty Common
Worcester
WR6 5UN
01886821403

Catherine.fuller@talk21.com

Phil Taylor qualified as an engineer before his career in the probation service. Between 1969 and 1999 he worked as a probation officer, manager and trainer. He continued working as a freelance trainer in all areas of the criminal justice sector until 2005. During his 15 years in training, Phil pioneered new ways of assessment for NVQs and wrote and published many colourful training packages in association with Linda Gast and Catherine Fuller. Phil is now retired and has returned to University to learn creative writing, for his own pleasure.

Acknowledgements

There are many people we would like to thank for their help and influence in writing this book, including:

William Miller and Stephen Rollnick for the theory and research into effective motivational interviewing.

Prochaska and Di Clemente for their ideas on the 'cycle of change' which has proved to be a useful, accessible framework to assist the application of motivational work.

James Sandham for introducing us to the practical application of motivational skills in the criminal justice sector.

Lin Taylor for ideas and support over the years and creatively laying out the materials.

Linda Gast for permission to update the chapter on rapport in *Influence and Integrity, A practice handbook for pro-social modelling,* by Linda Gast and Phil Taylor, originally published by MPTC Birmingham, 2002. Material from the *The Trainer's Pack for Pro-social Modelling* by the same authors is also included. Thanks are due to Linda and Phil for permission to publish this version. Enquiries regarding the above can be made to Linda and Mike Gast Training, e-mail: *training@lindagast.co.uk*

Tudor Williams for supporting our work over the years, demonstrations of motivational management and for permission to publish updated versions of material from the *Toolkit of Motivational skills (first edition) 2003, by Fuller, C., and Taylor, P., published by National Probation Directorate.*

Sally Cherry (Midlands Probation Training Consortium) and Mike Tennant (National Offender Management Services) for permission to publish updated versions of materials from *Systematic Motivational Skills for Approved Premises, 2004,* by Fuller, C., published by National Probation Directorate and Midlands Probation Consortium. Thanks are also due to Sally for her help in developing staff training in motivational skills in conjunction with Pro-Social Modelling.

Dave Thompson for his lively and appropriate illustrations.

Sue Jenner for her commentary on the Toolkit, demonstrating the spirit of motivational interviewing in so many interactions and help to develop motivational skills training both nationally and internationally.

Commissioners of training and participants on all our courses without whose examples of practical application this book would not have been written.

Chapter 1

Theoretical origins, rationale, techniques.

> 'It is the method and not the content that is the message...
> the drawing out, not the pumping in.'
>
> *Ashley Montagu*

INTRODUCTION

- How can you help someone who does not want to change a pattern of harmful behaviour?
- How can you help someone who wants to, but feels unable to change?
- How can you help someone who has started to change, continue to change?

These are questions that people helping others to change face everyday. It was struggling with these questions for over 20 years within criminal justice and education that inspired the authors to identify the elements of communication which are effective in helping someone to say, believe and act on: 'I want to, I can and I will change'.

Our experience was that within statutory agencies, a confrontational approach was still fairly common and that such an approach rarely helped people change behaviour in the long term. The more some people were told to keep appointments; warned they would go to prison; ordered to gain employment; advised to develop their basic skills; the more they resisted, challenged and continued to stay the same. On the other hand, where rapport was gained, where there was a genuine effort to understand, focus on self-determination and developing self-motivation, change was much more likely to occur.

Self-motivation is not a thing that can be given to someone: it needs to grow within each individual. What you can do is plant the seeds from which self-motivation can grow and nourish the environment. *The Toolkit of Motivational Skills* explores how the way you communicate can create an environment conducive to building self-motivation in others. The spirit and principles of a motivational approach are explored, followed by an outline of the key skills and how these can be used to respond to different stages of motivation to change. Step-by-step practical exercises are provided for you to develop your own skills and for you to use with the people you are helping to change. An electronic colour version of these exercises is provided at (www.wiley.com/go/motivationalskills) and can be adapted for your particular situation.

See **Chapter 5** for more on exploring current motivation.

Copies of the exercises can be downloaded from the website at **www.wiley.com/go/motivationalskills**

Without self-motivation, there is at worst resistance and at best hesitancy and compliance. Once there is self-motivation, all manner of things can be achieved, which may have seemed 'impossible' before. The scope of situations where there are benefits to developing self-motivation is vast. *The Toolkit of Motivational Skills* has been written primarily for front-line workers in health, social care, criminal justice and youth services. It will also be of benefit to parents, teachers, staff developers, counsellors, coaches and managers; indeed to any one who is helping someone else change. Most academic books on helping people to change have referred to 'therapists' or 'counsellors' and their 'clients'. We have not used this terminology, as the scope for the use of this book is wide. The people you are working with may not have paid for your services or even referred themselves to you for assistance. Your role may not be that of a therapist and you do not need qualifications in psychology, psychiatry, or counselling to integrate a motivational approach into your work. The skills are valuable for more formal interviews, but anyone can develop these skills and communicate more effectively in everyday conversations. We have used the terms 'interviewer' and 'interviewee' to refer to situations where a more formal interview may be present and 'facilitator' and 'service user' for a wider range of situations. Feel free to change the terminology to suit your own situation.

The motivational approach we propose is based on 'motivational interviewing' described by William Miller and Stephen Rollnick (1991, 2002). Our approach is true to the spirit and principles of Motivational Interviewing and has been adapted for practical, everyday application to many different situations.

In this chapter of the Toolkit you are provided with an overview of the motivational approach. The evidence for its effectiveness is discussed in Chapter 2. Practical ways to apply this are covered in the chapters which follow.

THE FIVE PRINCIPLES

> 'If someone goes into your house and moves the furniture around, the first thing you do is to move it all back again.'
>
> *Course participant*

Miller and Rollnick (2002, p. 25) describe motivational interviewing as a 'client centred, directive method for enhancing intrinsic motivation to change by exploring and resolving ambivalence.' We have identified five key principles around this definition. Miller and Rollnick's descriptions of these principles are added in (brackets) where this differs.

1. Clarify contracts (*additional principle to those identified by Miller and Rollnick*)
2. Express empathy
3. Develop desire to change (*develop discrepancy*)
4. Avoid argument (*roll with resistance*)
5. Support self-belief and self-responsibility (*self-efficacy*)

Clarify Contracts

The use of clear contracts allows, from the start, that the organisation, the worker, and service user may not share all the same expectations

See **Chapter 4** for more on making contracts

or goals and makes these explicit in order to find collaborative common ground. To be conducive to self-motivation the contract is jointly owned.

A good starting point is for both the worker and the service user to ask:

'How come I am working with this person towards change?'

To fully answer this question requires you to have a clear understanding of the working relationship between yourself and the other person. This will vary widely depending on the circumstances and the agency you work for. The words you use to describe the person you work with will reflect this relationship, for example, 'patient'; 'friend'; 'service user'; 'offender'; 'student'; 'colleague'. Each of these implies different expectations and boundaries. A detailed discussion of contracts is provided in Chapter 4.

Both Chris Trotter (1999) and Sue Rex (Rex and Matravers 1998) highlight the difference that a clear agreement about roles, expectations, boundaries and outcomes makes to the completion of court orders; authority is more accepted as legitimate and commitment to change is increased. Similarly, Miller and Rollnick (2002) discuss contracting as the starting point for working with people who want to change.

Express Empathy

An accurate understanding of the particular needs of each individual who is considering change is sought, without judging, criticising, labelling or blaming. Empathy is particularly associated with client-centred therapy (Rogers 1951), but has also been successfully incorporated into most other approaches which

> See **Chapters 4, 7 and 8** for more on building empathy

help people to change. Luborsky et al. (1985) and Miller et al. (1980) found that the degree of empathy experienced by service users accounted for behaviour change significantly more than the type of counselling method. The skills for building accurate empathy are explored in Chapters 4 and 7.

Develop Desire to Change (*Develop Discrepancy*)

Unlike a pure client-centred counsellor (Rogers 1951), the motivational facilitator

> See **Chapters 11 and 12** for more on developing the desire to change

guides the service user towards considering change by drawing out how present behaviour conflicts with longer term values or goals. Miller and Rollnick (2002) refer to this as 'developing discrepancy'.

The art of developing discrepancy is to gently highlight and reflect back inconsistencies or discrepancies in what has been said.

The aim of a motivational approach is for people to identify their own reasons to change; not for the facilitator to impose their reasons. It is the difference between 'intrinsic' motivation, which comes from within and 'extrinsic' motivation, which needs external rewards or threats. For example, developing the desire to stop offending in order to be a good father, is only effective if the person who is considering change, really wants to be a good father.

The motivational approach is more 'directive' than a pure client-centred approach, which would not selectively highlight inconsistencies between long-term and short-term goals in the same way. However, unlike a confrontational approach, the facilitator does not try to impose this direction by insisting or trying to persuade the service user to take a certain course of action. Decisions are ultimately chosen by the service user.

The concept of developing discrepancy is similar to the cognitive behaviourist ideas of 'cognitive dissonance' introduced by Festinger (1957), who found that where people became aware that their behaviour conflicted with their values and beliefs they were more likely to want to change in order to reduce the discomfort. Evidence for this intrinsic motivation supporting long-term change more than extrinsic rewards and sanctions, is provided by Kohn (2000) and Deci and Ryan (1987), who found that behaviour which is reinforced only by rewards tended to stop when the rewards stop.

Avoid Argument (Roll with Resistance)

If you think about your interactions with the people you help to change there may well be some situations where you seem to

See **Chapter 10** for more on working with resistance

be doing all the work; where you are constantly presenting arguments and reasons to change and they are constantly arguing back all the reasons to stay the same. In such situations it can be easy to label such people 'resistant,' 'in denial' or 'difficult'. A motivational approach sees resistance as a normal part of the change process and is linked with feeling uncertain or 'ambivalent' about change. If resistance starts to increase during the interview, this is a sign for the facilitator to change the style of communication and to listen, reflect understanding and explore. Once the service user has exhausted all the reasons not to change, reasons to change can be explored and inconsistencies gently highlighted. In this way, you 'roll with resistance' (Gordon 1970).

A motivational approach seems to work by reducing negativity. Research by Miller, Benefield and Tonigan (1993) explored the details of what people said to their therapists and the subsequent behaviour change. The research supports the idea that the more people say they won't change and give reasons to stay the same the more this is likely to become a reality. By trying to persuade, the facilitator can ironically, make it more likely that the person will stay the same. When the facilitator behaves in a way that does not lead to resistance, change is much more likely to follow.

Support Self-belief and Self-responsibility (Self-efficacy)

The facilitator guides the service user to identify how to 'resolve the ambivalence' and overcome the barriers to change. The service user is encouraged to believe in the possibility of change and to take self-responsibility for change (self-efficacy).

See **Chapters 13 and 14** for more on self-belief and self-responsibility

The principle of self-responsibility is supported by the cognitive behavioural work of Bandura (1977) and client-centred work of Rogers (1969), which both found that the more you believe you can achieve something, the more likely you are to take on higher level tasks and the more likely you are to achieve them. There is evidence that the facilitator's belief in the possibility of change is also a contributing factor (Leake and King 1977), whether this is labelling someone negatively as a 'failure', an 'alcoholic' or an 'addict' or positively as capable of achieving change. Rosenthal and Jacobson (1992) have referred to this as the 'Pygmalion' effect.

THE KEY MOTIVATIONAL SKILLS

> 'For a person to feel responsible for his actions he must sense that his behaviour has flowed from the self.'
>
> *Stanley Milgram*

All change involves a loss
- **A**ffirm
- **L**isten
- **O**pen questions
- **S**ummarise and Reflect
- **S**upport self-motivating statements

The key skills most associated with the five principles of a motivational approach are to: **A**ffirm, **L**isten, use **O**pen questions, **S**ummarise and **S**upport self-motivating statements.

In any encounter between people, each affects the behaviour of the other. The extent to which this is a relation of common accord we call *Rapport.* All of the above skills both build rapport and depend upon it. Chapter 4 explores the interactive nature of all human communication and some of the ways in which they can be made more effective. The underlying principle is:

> 'The meaning of your communication is the response you get. If you are not getting the response you want, change what you are doing.'
>
> *Laborde 1987, p. 207*

None of the skills are miracle techniques to 'use on people' to produce change. Without the spirit of motivational work they may indeed produce the opposite effect. Of all the skills the most important is listening. Without listening, the others will not amount to a motivational approach. The acronym for recalling the skills, 'A LOSS', serves as a reminder that all change involves loss and this needs to be recognised when working towards change.

Affirm (Build Self-belief)

Client-centred therapy suggests that people are more likely to change if they feel good about themselves and are affirmed (Rogers 1951). To affirm someone, is to work with them in a way that builds their self-belief and self-confidence. Someone who is affirmed feels that they are a valuable human being. Affirmation is especially important at the beginning of a working relationship when empathy is sought. At the start, affirmation is expressed by how you greet service users, use their name, gain raport, respect their differences and help them to feel welcome and listened to. Throughout, you affirm someone by not labelling them and valuing them as an individual.

See **Chapter 13** for more on affirmation

Trotter (1999) found that on average, in order to accept one criticism you need to hear at least five positive affirmations about your behaviour. Many service users have experienced a balance very much the other way. Any criticism within the interview may therefore produce resistance. Criticism, disapproval, ridicule and punishment are not used within motivational interviewing. Affirmation on the other hands builds self-belief, self-responsibility and self-efficacy.

Listen

Listening is an essential ingredient of all five motivational principles. We all think we can listen, however, in practice we often have competing demands and distractions. To listen and observe well is a skill that needs time, commitment and practise. Listening is not about not talking, nor is it just hearing the words, it is about gaining a genuine understanding of the person from what they are enabled to tell us (empathy). Only by

See **Chapter 7** for more on listening skills

higher level listening will longer term values and the conflicts with present behaviour be heard (develop discrepancy). Many of the people you work with may have had a 'good talking to', but may never have experienced a 'good listening to'.

Approximatly 92% of communication is non-verbal or tone (pitch and volume) of voice (Mehrabian 1972). Listening is both seeing and hearing all communication.

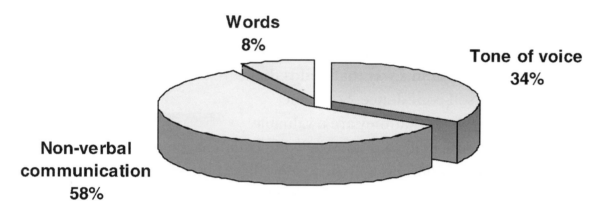

When establishing clear, jointly owned contracts, the service user's body language and tone of voice will provide an indication of whether they feel listened to and jointly involved.

Open Questions

Open questions are questions that cannot be answered with the words 'yes' or 'no'. The most helpful open questions often start with 'What…', 'Tell me…', 'Explain to me what…', or 'Describe what…'

See **Chapter 9** for more on using open questions

How? When? Where? Which? Who? and Why? are also open questions, and Chapter 9 explores how some are more helpful than others. The integration of open questions into a dialogue can be a useful way to draw out more information and increase the desire to change. In order to be motivational, questions need to be asked in a context of the other skills of listening and reflecting and within the spirit of empathy and developing self-efficacy. Several studies (Lambert 1976) have indicated that when used on their own as a cold technique, open questions are not conducive to self-motivation. A question is defined by the *Oxford English Dictionary* as an 'interrogative sentence' and questions can be experienced as an interrogation. However, relatively few, or even just one, pertinent question combined with high level reflective listening can be the catalyst to building desire and confidence to change (self-efficacy). Miller and Rollnick (2002) suggest limiting questions and their answers to no more than three in a row.

Summarise and Reflect Listening

The essence of reflective listening is that it enables you to guess at what the person means and then summarise this as a statement, 'So you mean…' rather than use a closed question 'Do you mean?' The service user does not feel interrogated; they feel understood and thus more likely to provide further information.

> See **Chapter 8** for more on summarising and reflections

Summaries can occur immediately after the service user has spoken or at the end of period of discussion. They can range from simple reflections of what the service user has said, to reflections of perceived meaning and feelings, to more complex summaries which highlight inconsistencies. Each of these has a different effect and is explored further in Chapter 8.

The use of skilful summaries can:

- Encourage the speaker to say more and enable you to clarify understanding, thereby enhancing accurate empathy.
- Develop discrepancy by emphasising inconsistencies the service user has mentioned between current behaviour and long-term goals or values.
- Demonstrate that you are listening and accept arguments, without necessarily agreeing, and thereby reduce resistance.
- Ensure you are working only with the material that has been offered and which is owned by the service user; thereby encouraging self-responsibility and self-belief.
- Clarify areas of agreement and facilitate clear contracts.

Support self-motivating statements

Self-motivating statements are a key ingredient for clear contracts, developing discrepancy and self-belief in change.

> See **Chapter 12 and 13** for more on self-motivating statements

A self-motivating statement always comes from the service user, states a positive desire, confidence or willingness to do something and includes personal ownership , the word 'I' is used for instance:

- 'I want to change'
- 'I can change'
- 'I will change'.

I want to   I can   I will

The emphasis is on the service user voicing the desire or confidence to change, not the facilitator. In this respect a motivational approach builds on Bem's self-perception theory (Bem 1972), which states that we tend to believe what we hear ourselves say.

Amrhein et al.'s (2003) psycholinguistic research indicated that the most effective self-motivating statements demonstrated high levels of a:

- Need to change
- Desire to change
- Reasons to change
- Ability to change
- Commitment to change.

There was significantly more impact on future behaviour when this 'commitment language' increased in intensity and quality towards the end of the session rather than decreased during the session.

A CYCLE OF CHANGE

How the skills and principles are used varies according to how ready someone is to change. Prochaska and DiClemente's (1982) research into behaviour change within the field of 'addictive' behaviours provides a

See **Chapter 6** for more on the cycle of change

useful complementary model for applying a motivational approach and identifying when alternative approaches may be useful.

The stages of change Prochaska and DiClemente describe, have been presented diagrammatically in a number of different ways. We have found six stages as part of the same cycle to be the most helpful.

Their 'transtheoretical' model of change is described as a 'personal pathway through the stages and helps understand the multiple influences involved in the acquisition and cessation of addictions' (DiClemente 2006, p.19.). We have found that the concepts apply equally well to other situations where people struggle with change. Heather (1996) found that a motivational approach was particularly effective in comparison with behaviourist approaches at the earlier stages of pre-contemplation and contemplation. DiClemente and Velasquez (in Miller and Rollnick 2002)

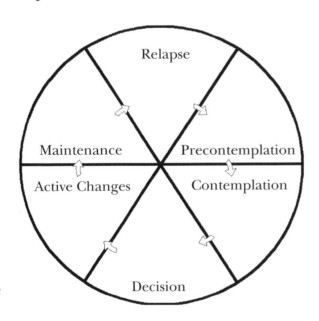

have also found these stages to be the most suited to motivational work, whilst also identifying how a motivational approach can enhance other approaches at later stages. Any individual you are working with could be at one stage for one sort of behaviour, another for other behaviour or be moving between stages.

Pre-contemplation

At pre-contemplation, change is not being considered. Other people may think someone has a problem, but that person does not. Examples would include a person, who is:

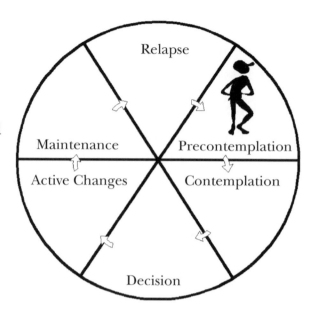

- Taking large quantities of drugs or alcohol, which are adversely effecting behaviour and health
- Eating inadequately to maintain good health
- Truanting from school
- Not taking prescribed drugs
- Committing offences frequently.

A motivational approach aims to gradually initiate the consideration of change. Empathy and associated skills of listening and summarising are especially useful at the pre-contemplation stage. The use of additional principles and skills will vary according to the reason someone is pre-contemplational. Someone who is reluctant to change through lack of knowledge may respond well to the provision of new information in addition to motivational skills. Those who are rebellious about change may treat new information as fuel for further argument. The latter may respond better to someone who rolls with resistance, listens and reflects understanding.

See **Chapter 10** for more on pre-contemplation and resistance

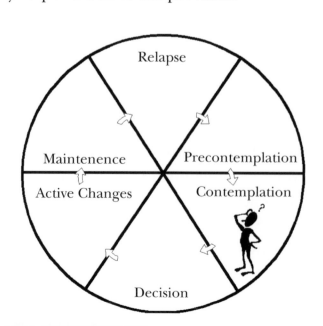

Contemplation

Seeds of doubt have been sown. The service user is aware of some of the advantages of change and the disadvantages of their present behaviour. However, a clear decision to change has not been made; they enjoy their current behaviour and know it will be difficult to change. It is almost as if there are four voices

See **Chapter 11** for more on ambivalence and motivational balance

in the head constantly arguing for and against change. The ambivalence this produces can lead to confusion and inactivity or continuation with the problematic behaviour as the easiest option.

A motivational approach at this stage aims to help the individual explore and resolve ambivalence without trying to impose change. The motivational balance (Janis and Mann 1977) is a useful tool for exploring the pros and cons of change and of staying the same.

Costs of staying the same

Gains of change

Gains of staying the same

Costs of change

At contemplation stage all the key motivational principles and skills are used. It may be tempting to start telling or teaching new behaviours at this stage, however, there is ample research which indicates that this can be counterproductive. Colin Roberts's (2003) research into the 'Think First' accredited programme for offenders indicates that time and resources can be wasted by trying to force people to change at this stage. He found that people who started, but were not motivated to complete programmes re-offended more frequently than those who did not start at all. The typical reaction to being pushed into change is to rebel against the advice. A motivational approach listens to the barriers to change without judgement and gradually helps others voice the reason for and confidence to change themselves.

Decision

When there is a clear decision to
change you will hear increased
self-motivating language and
reduced resistance talk. You will
hear such phrases as:

- 'I want to change because…'
- 'I can change because…'
- 'I will start changing…'
- 'I am ready to start now…'

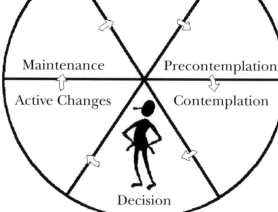

There is a willingness to make
clear contracts for change and
explore with you how to overcome any
barriers.

See **Chapter 14**
for more on the
decision stage

The art of the motivational approach
is to assess whether someone is ready for
change now, and to nurture their early
intimations of change. Revisiting the values and goals identified when
developing discrepancy is helpful, as is developing self-belief in the
possibility of change. The mistake is to rush
into action planning too quickly. Ideas for
change are initially sought from the person
changing and supplemented with new
information, where helpful. In the desire to

See **Chapter 5**
for more on exploring
current motivation

achieve change you may find that you frequently judge the decision stage
to have arrived earlier than it has. Where action plans are made prior to a
genuine decision they are generally not kept to. Within statutory settings,
staff may be required to make contracts and plans when the service user is
still pre-contemplational about change. The key is to only include actions
that focus on the work to be undertaken in the pre-contemplation and
contemplation stage. The plan could be to explore the desirability of
change and benefits of staying the same, plus any areas the service user is
currently motivated to work on.

When someone is at the action stage they have started to take small steps towards change. A motivational approach is to listen and affirm. Rather than providing material rewards and sanctions you will provide verbal praise and affirmations. Deci and Ryan (1985) found the following rewards to be most effective:

See **Chapter 13** for more on the confidence to change

- verbal (rather than materialistic)
- specific to identifiable behaviour
- genuine, owned and supported by non-verbal communication
- unexpected
- informative rather than controlling.

Additional skills from other disciplines of providing information and actively helping may also be helpful. When combined with a motivational approach these skills focus on choice and self-determination. West (1990) found that the way in which advice is given makes a significant difference. She found that where doctors presented advice in the form of information or feedback and possible options, this was acted on significantly more often than when it was presented as a command or value judgement.

Action

At the action stage, actively helping someone to overcome barriers can be very effective. Kogan (1957) found that making the contact phone call for an appointment with the service user in the office can more than double the chance of the referral being completed. Other examples would be verbal reminders of appointments, assistance with arranging transport and help with using the telephone or completing forms if someone has literacy problems.

See **Chapter 15** for more on supporting change

Removing the barriers will only be effective if the service user wants them removed; whilst effective at action stage, it may not be at contemplation stage.

Maintenance

At the maintenance stage change has occurred over a period of time. This is usually considered to be over six months or more. Cognitive behaviourist methods also work well at this stage and can be used in conjunction with motivational skills to assist the service user to:

- affirm progress and build confidence
- identify risky situations which may lead to lapse and strategies to overcome these
- develop new skills and behaviours
- leave the cycle altogether and build a new life.

Lapse

Prochaska and DiClemente (1982) found that smokers tended to go around the cycle on average seven times before change occurred. Lapse is a normal part of the change cycle. People react to lapse in different ways. Disappointment, anger, guilt and loss of hope can lead to a more long-term relapse. A motivational worker affirms the person who has lapsed and returns with them to contemplation to re-establish optimism.

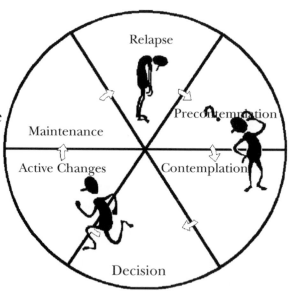

What motivates someone to change and which interventions they respond to, depends partly on where they are on the cycle of change. What helps someone to start thinking about change can be different from what helps someone initiate and maintain action. Motivational principles and skills are particularly effective when working with people who are pre-contemplational or contemplational about their current behaviour.

SUMMARY OF A MOTIVATIONAL APPROACH

How the facilitator communicates, has the potential to increase motivation, but it also has the potential to reduce it (see Table 1.1 below). The meaning of your communication is the response you get.

Table 1.1 How communication can effect motivation

To increase motivation:	To reduce motivation:
Principles	**Principles**
• Clarify and agree contracts • Seek empathy • Develop desire to change/discrepancy • Avoid argument: Roll with resistance • Support self-belief and responsibility.	• Do not clarify expectations • Treat everyone the same • Collude: 'I would do the same' • Confront: 'I'm right, you're wrong' • Make all the decisions.
Core skills:	**Core skills:**
• Affirm, praise positive behaviours • Listen • Ask open infrequent questions • Summarise and reflect • Support self-motivating statements.	• Point out faults • Tell • Ask closed or frequent questions • Warn and threaten • Advise and persuade.
Process:	**Process:**
• Build rapport, contract • Respond to motivation • *Pre-contemplation:* Raise doubt • *Contemplation:* Develop desire and confidence to change • *Decision:* Joint plans • *Action, Lapse and Maintenance* Support change, learn from lapse.	• Ignore building rapport • Assume everyone is motivated • Start with plans to change behaviour • Label those negatively, who do not comply • Label lapse as 'failure' • Punish those who fail. Prepare to 'let go'
Service user's response	**Service user's response**
Increasing commitment: 'I ought to, but...', becomes 'I want to', becomes 'I want to because...', becomes 'I can', becomes **'I will!'**	Increasing resistance: 'I ought to, but...', becomes 'I don't want to', becomes 'I don't want to because...', becomes 'I can't', becomes **'I won't!'**

SUMMARY

In essence the theory behind a motivational approach is that the more you use motivational principles, the more likely your service users are to express increasing commitment. If expressed commitment increases in intensity during a session, change is more likely; if it reduces, change what you are doing. The next chapter examines the evidence for the effectiveness of a motivational approach.

- What are the advantages of examining the evidence for the effectiveness of your practice?
- What are the risks if you don't?
- What difference will it make to your practice if you adopt an approach that is backed by evidence of effectiveness?

These are questions you may wish to ask yourself before reading this chapter. Front line workers use a variety of approaches to try to help others change, which are sometimes determined by personal preference or organisational custom. The authors have adopted a motivational approach not only because it fits with their value base, but also because there is considerable evidence that it works.

In this chapter we ask a number of questions concerning the effectiveness of the motivational approach and provide sign posts to direct you to more detailed research studies.

SUMMARY OF EVIDENCE

What Evidence is There That a Motivational Approach Helps People to Change?

A number of studies indicate that a motivational approach assists change significantly more than no intervention, particularly in relation to substance abuse and diet control.

(Miller and Rollnick (2002), and meta-analysis of a total of 100 studies by Burke et al. (2003) and Hettema et al. (2004)).

The motivational approach was originally used and researched within the field of addictive behaviours. In recent years it has been widely used within the health and criminal justice services, including helping people to: stick to programmes of prescribed drugs, keep appointments, attend treatment programmes, control insulin intake and maintain diets. There is less research into the effectiveness of the approach within these areas, but what there is looks promising.

How Much More Effective is a Motivational Approach than Other Approaches?

> The greatest evidence for the effectiveness of a motivational approach is in comparison with *confrontational approaches.*

- Confrontation has been found to exacerbate alcohol intake, whilst motivational styles have reduced intake (Miller et al. 1993).
- Drop out rates from treatment programmes tend to increase in response to a confrontational style and decrease in response to a motivational style. (Miller et al. 1993, 2003).
- Confronting sex offenders can lead to protection of self-image and limited disclosure, whilst a motivational approach is more likely to lead to engagement in therapy (Kear-Colwell and Pollock (1997); Mann and Rollnick (1996).

> Motivational approaches have been found to be more effective than self-help or education methods.

Gambling (Hodgins et al. 2001) reduced and condom use by patients with HIV increased (Belcher et al. 1988) significantly more in response to a motivational approach than in response to self-help or education.

> Motivational approaches can be more effective long term than behaviourist methods, particularly where there is ambivalence about change.

Deci and Ryan (1985) found that motivational approaches enhanced intrinsic motivation and long-term change. Heather et al. (1996) found that, where a clear decision to change had been made, a behaviourist style was just as effective as a motivational style. However, a motivational style was significantly more effective than a behaviourist style, where there was ambivalence about change.

> Punishment may produce short-term compliance, but longer term it increases behaviour problems; whilst a motivational approach can produce commitment to long-term change.

Lipsey (1992) found that punishments such as intensive surveillance and shock incarceration led to a 25% increase in reoffending rates compared with a control group. Gershoff (2002) provides a comprehensive analysis of the effects of punishment in a range of situations and comes to a similar conclusion. Where punishment does produce compliance it is short-term and the old behaviour tends to return when the punishment is withdrawn. A motivational approach aims for more than compliance; it aims for a commitment to long term-change.

> There remains less evidence of the efficacy of motivational work in comparison with *cognitive behaviourist* and *client-centred approaches.*

Motivational interviewing contains elements of cognitive behaviourist and client-centred approaches and therefore it is not surprising that there is less evidence of the effectiveness of motivational interviewing in comparison with them. Dowden and Andrew's (2004) meta-analysis of 270 studies found that very few pieces of research into such programmes could identify enough detail of how the programme was delivered to differentiate them. The studies by Sellman et al. (2001) and Kemp (1998) are exceptions; they demonstrated the added value of motivational interviewing over non-directive client-centred approaches for alcohol outpatients and people with psychosis respectively. Project MATCH (Project MATCH Research Group 1997) is one of the most comprehensive pieces of research comparing the impact of cognitive behaviourist methods, a medical model and an adaptation of motivational interviewing on the alcohol use of almost 2,000 people. All three approaches were found to be effective.

> The motivational approach was as effective as a cognitive and client-centred approach in the shortest amount of time.

How Effective is a Motivational Approach in Combination with Other Approaches?

> A motivational approach works well in preparation for other treatment or in combination with other approaches.

The following studies are examples of the evidence of the added value of motivational interviewing in conjunction with other approaches.

- Barrowclough et al. (2001) found that *dual diagnosis* patients were significantly more likely to change if they were provided with motivational interviewing sessions and a cognitive behaviourist programme, than if they just experienced the cognitive behaviourist programme.
- Resnicow et al. (2002) found that the patients who received *health education* and a session of motivational interviewing were significantly more likely to increase their intake of fruit and vegetables than those who received health education alone.
- Scales (1995) found that patients who received information on *cardiovascular rehabilitation* and motivational interviewing sessions were significantly more likely to experience a reduction in stress and increase physical activity, than those who received information alone.

- Smith et al. (1997) found that patients with *diabetes* were significantly more likely to improve self-monitoring of glucose intake and control their weight if they received both a motivational interviewing session and a behavioural programme, than if they just experienced the behavioural programme.

- The use of a motivational approach in preparation for other treatment would seem to be particularly useful if the alternative is a *'waiting list'*. Several studies have found that waiting lists become self-fulfilling prophesies with less action being taken even in comparison with no treatment (Harris and Miller 1990).

IMPLICATIONS FOR PRACTICE

When is a Motivational Approach not Appropriate?

Where there is *immediate danger* to the service user or to others the approach may be questionable.

Within a residential setting, for instance, if a service user was about to hurt someone else, aspects of the motivational interviewing approach may be used such as remaining calm and diffusing the situation in conjunction with aspects of a more controlling approach. A service user who has been sectioned under the mental health act, or one who is suffering an acute episode of illness, may not be in a position to respond to talk therapy. They may respond in the shorter term to a medical approach, especially if there is an immediate danger. Treasure and Ward (1997) for instance, have questioned the use of motivational interviewing with patients with eating disorders, if their lives are in immediate danger.

The use of the whole motivational approach is not always necessary.

If a service user is in distress the most appropriate intervention may be counselling with none of the elements of direction towards change.

Rollnick (2003) agrees that the approach is not always appropriate and gives the example of a child running into the road. The parent's initial response may be controlling or, if the child is hurt, supportive. A motivational approach of exploring alternatives and empowering for change may occur at a later time.

A motivational interviewing style is also questionable where the service user is:

- responding well to other methods
- actively changing already
- increasing the frequency and strength of resistance talk and reducing the use of self-motivating statements in response to motivational interviewing.

Miller and Rollnick (2002, pp.161-179) have questioned the ethics and whether the techniques can be delivered within the spirit of motivational interviewing when there is a:

- strong emotional or vested interest by the worker in achieving change quickly
- poor or 'dissonant' relationship between facilitator and service user
- lack of understanding or commitment to the spirit of motivational interviewing and some skills (such as questioning) are used in isolation.

When is a Motivational Approach Most Appropriate?

A motivational approach seems to be most appropriate in comparison with other methods where the service user is:

- ambivalent about change (Heather *et al.*, 1996)
- unresponsive or resistant to other method (Project MATCH Research Group, 1997)
- initially aggressive, resistant or uncommunicative (Prochaska and DiClemente, 1982)
- waiting for another treatment programme (Barrowclough *et al.*, 2001)
- where you hear evidence of the service user's resistance talk reducing and self-motivating statements increasing during the motivational interaction.

How Applicable is a Motivational Approach to Practice?

Harper and Hardy (2000) found that a number of practitioners were concerned that motivational interviewing might be too time consuming and complex. It is in response to this criticism that this book has been written.

> Aspects of the approach can be adopted by any staff helping others to change, from a 20-second intervention onwards.

Lengthy interviews over a long period of time are not necessary. Monti et al. (1999) found that a single 35 minute motivational session significantly reduced several key alcohol related problems in the six months which followed. Burke et al. (2003) found that on average one-four sessions made a significant impact on future behaviour and Woollard and colleagues (1995) found little difference in outcomes between hypertensive patients who received six high intensity motivational interviewing session with those who received a single session.

This is not to say that a motivational approach is simply a set of techniques. The provision of prepared scripts for delivery (Dilorio et al. 2003) is not in itself motivational. The spirit of the approach, a genuine desire to understand, respond to difference and empower others to change, is more important than any technique. The journey to develop this motivational spirit is one that never ends. However, from your first step on this journey, the response you receive from others starts to change.

How will this Toolkit Help You to Help Others?

The Toolkit goes further than providing prepared scripts, but does not insist on post-graduate understanding of psychology for delivery. The aim of the Toolkit is to outline the essence of the theory and provide practical, easy to access strategies for everyday use. The Toolkit draws on our experience of training hundreds of workers and what they have told us worked for them.

In the following chapters motivational principles and skills are unpacked in simple language, with lots of examples for application. Chapter 3 starts this process by exploring how you can use the Toolkit to meet the many different needs of the people with whom you work.

Motivational work seeks to understand and respond effectively to each individual in order for them to achieve change. This chapter provides an overview of how the Toolkit can help you to achieve this. It offers signposts to the some of the important differences between individuals and gives suggestions to adapt the materials provided so as to respond to those differences.

Every person is like all other persons, is only like some other person and is also like no other person.

I need to know what this is all about.

In some respects everyone you work with is unique and the response you get from an intervention with one person will never be exactly the same as the response you get from another. An essential starting point is therefore to gain empathy and rapport with each person you work with. The skills to build this rapport are explored in **Chapter 4 – Establishing Rapport and Making Contracts.**

In other respects the individuals you work with will have similarities with some people, but not with others. We have seen how research indicates that an individual's stage of motivation is a significant factor in determining how they will respond to interventions. The Toolkit provides examples of effective communication for change at each of these stages.

Chapter 5 – Exploring Current Motivation will help you to start to explore motivation with each person you work with and to ensure your approach is appropriate for each individual.

what is my motivation?

Chapter 6 – The Cycle of Change provides exercises to help you and the service user make a more accurate assessment of which stage of motivation is relevant for a particular behaviour, and how best to work towards the next stage.

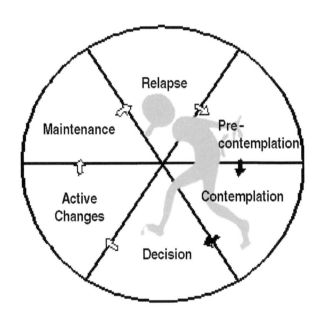

Chapter 7 – Listening Skills, Chapter 8 – Summarising and Reflective Listening and Chapter 9 – Asking Open Questions, will help you to develop these three key motivational skills, which are used in different ways to build and maintain motivation to change.

This guy is really listening to me.

Chapter10 – Working with Resistance will help you to make a positive response to resistance to change that can enable the service user to move on. At the pre-contemplation stage a skilful response to resistance can sow seeds of doubts about the stuck behaviour.

Chapter 11 – Exploring Ambivalence provides exercises to use with service users to nourish the seeds of doubt sown and explore the ambivalence which results (early contemplation stage).

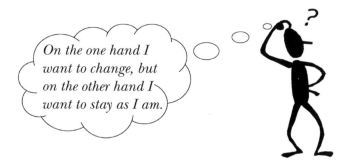

Chapter 12 – Developing the Desire to Change provides you with ideas to help service users resolve ambivalence in favour of change (middle contemplation stage).

Chapter 13 – Affirmation and Confidence to Change will help you build confidence in service users who want to change but don't yet feel they have the confidence to make a start (later contemplation stage and also relevant to decision, action, maintenance stages).

Chapter 14 – Motivational Action Planning provides you and service users with exercises to assist action planning once a firm decision to change has been reached (decision stage).

I want to, I can and I will change, now

Chapter 15 – Supporting Change provides you and service users with exercises and ideas to maintain change and to recover from any lapses occurring in the journey (action, (re)lapse and maintenance stages).

Finally, in some respects everyone you work with is the same in that they all share fluctuating stages of motivation. The majority will respond to empathy; gently developing a sense of discrepancy between long-term goals and short-term behaviour, avoiding argument, and supporting self-belief and self-responsibility.

I have changed, and can stay changed.

Chapter 16 – Putting it all Together; Cultivating your Skills will help you to develop these principles in your everyday work so that you can respond motivationally, with more confidence and more skill to a variety of different situations.

Key Skills

THE TOOLKIT AND LEARNING

The Toolkit has been designed to meet the needs of different readers and different service users. Kolb (1984) found that most effective learning takes place when people:

1. use 'here and now' examples
2. reflect on experiences
3. apply learning from one situation to another and relate to general principles
4. rehearse and plan how to apply learning.

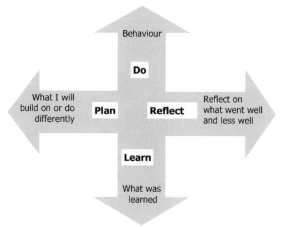

Honey and Mumford (1986) further found that people have a preference to start this cycle of learning at one of four different points, to first:

1. understand the theory (*theorists*), or
2. identify how it is relevant to their practice (*pragmatists*), or
3. try out new experiences (*activists*), or
4. reflect on their existing practice (*reflectors*).

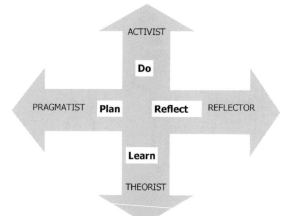

The Toolkit includes all aspects of the learning cycle and takes into account different preferences for starting points.

☑ It can be read to reflect on existing practice
☑ It can be used to explore research and theoretical understanding and make connections with your other work
☑ It can be used to plan how you will change your change practice
☑ It can be used to select an exercise to use in response to a specific issue.

As you develop your motivational skills you may find it helpful to identify how you prefer to learn and how this effects your communication when working with others who have different learning styles. With practice you can improve the skills in the styles that are a lower preference for you, in order to meet the learning needs of those you work with (see Honey and Mumford 1986).

- An *activist style* is most helpful when working at the *action stage*
- A *reflector style* is useful at *pre-contemplation* and early contemplation in helping service users to start to think about their current behaviour. It can also be helpful at *relapse* to help service users identify what went well and less well the last time they made a change.
- A *theorist style* is useful at *contemplation* in enabling service users to identify reasons to change and to see connections with their other behaviour.
- A *pragmatist style* is helpful at *decision stage* in making plans to change behaviour and planning how to build new behaviours at the *maintenance stage.*

PREFERRED SENSE

Another important learning style is the individual's preferred use of their senses in learning about and describing their world.

Visual people take in information best through their eyes. They are helped by writing and pictures. They remember in pictures, some in full colour and great detail. The language they use contains many seeing words, for example 'I see what you mean.' 'That looks good to me.' 'I get the picture.'

Using visual language when talking to them, helps build rapport. In the face of excessive verbal explanations, they simply turn off. Hence this book has many pictures. The written exercises, when completed enable the service user to take a 'look' at their situation. When they write something down it becomes real to them.

Auditory people take in information best when listening. They also like to work out their ideas by talking about them with others. Unlike some visual people, they can respond well to work conducted in a traditional interview. They use auditory language, for example 'I hear what you say.' 'It's music to my ears.' 'That sounds good to me.' Using auditory language helps build rapport. They may be turned off by too much paper work. Some people cannot form any pictures in their minds; others may only have fuzzy pictures. This book has lots of skills which can be expressed verbally. When an Auditory person says something, it becomes real to them.

Kinaesthetic (feeling) people take in information best through their physical senses, experiencing what it feels like. It's almost as if there was an imprint of the physical activity, or the sensual experience in their brain hence, 'flying by the seat of their pants.' What does smoking feel like in the lungs and nose? Kinaesthetic people also refer to emotions. What they feel about something is very important to what they decide to do. Kinaesthetic people use feeling words, such as 'Let's get to grips with this.' 'That feels good to me.' 'It made no impact on me.' Using feeling language helps build rapport. This book suggests activities that might be undertaken to give learning experiences. It also builds skills to draw out and work with feelings. What a Kinaesthetic person feels is real to them.

Most people learn best when there is a combination of senses in use. Their dominant sense is then reinforced by the other senses. However, if a Visual person is asked to work without any visual input they will be in difficulty. Similarly for Auditory and Kinaesthetic people. Good practice, therefore, is to ensure you always use a variety of senses in every piece of work. Once you notice the dominant sense of your service user, you can improve rapport by focusing communication around that sense.

ADAPTING MATERIALS TO MEET INDIVIDUAL REQUIREMENTS

There are many other differences your services users will have including the following:

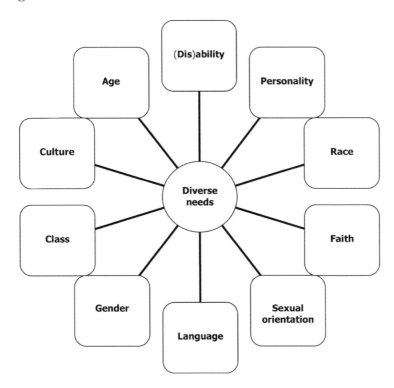

Everyone has a place in *every* box. A white, heterosexual woman, for instance, will experience the world very differently from a black lesbian woman. Within each of these areas you may find it helpful to:

☑ Change the imagery so that it reflects the service user's gender, faith, etc.
☑ Change verbal examples used so that they reflect sexual orientation, culture, age, etc.

- ☑ Adapt exercises involving images, speaking/listening or movement/touch to take into account individual's sensory abilities and preference
- ☑ Adapt your communication to respond to different levels of understanding
- ☑ Be aware of cultural expectations which are likely to help the service user feel more comfortable
- ☑ Use professional interpreters and advisors where required.

USING THE EXERCISES

The exercises for facilitators and for service users have been designed to appeal to a wide range of styles and circumstances. They can be easily located throughout the Toolkit by looking for the appropriate symbol and can also be found in colour on the website (www.wiley.com/go/motivationalskills). The exercises can be adapted to meet the different needs of your organisation and different service users by changing the wording and imagery or by discussing the content with service users.

The exercises below provide examples and frameworks for you to identify how you can adapt some of the material to your work.

The *first exercise* considers how to change language used for service users who have reading ages under 11. You may wish to change the language in this way if you are working with younger people, or people who have low basic skills. The end result will be different in each of these cases.

A significant proportion of adults supervised by criminal justice agencies have difficulties understanding complex language, yet many of the materials provided are geared to a much higher level of understanding. Many people in organisations use 'jargon' and abbreviations that people outside of their organisation do not understand. How true is this in your organisation?

The *second exercise* sheet may be used to reflect on existing practise in terms of responding to different needs or for you to keep a record of approaches that have worked for other people.

The *third exercise* aims to help you explore your practice in more detail in relation to two specific learners with very different needs.

You are asked to:
- Plan how you will respond to those needs (*pragmatist style*)
- Put this into practice (*action style*)
- Reflect on what worked well and less well (*reflector style*)
- Identify what you learnt from the experience (*theorist style*).

You may wish to take some time over this exercise and come back to it throughout the time you are helping someone to change. You can adapt the exercise to allow yourself more space for ideas or to reflect on work you have already done.

Facilitator's Worksheet F3.1: Getting the Message Across

Identify technical jargon or complex language you use in your work and the everyday ways of saying them. Where you want to use words with three or more beats or 'syl-la-bles', it is sometimes helpful to provide a simple explanation prior to the introduction of the new word as we have illustrated in this sentence. An example is provided first.

Examples of technical/ complex words	Examples of everyday ways of saying them
Motivated	I want to, I can, I will
Anticipate consequences	Think ahead and ask what is likely to happen
Different perspectives	See things from the other person's points of view
Ambivalence	Mixed feelings – unsure
Syllables	Beats
Develop discrepancy	Help someone see the difference between what they are doing now and what they really want in life
Self-efficacy	Belief that I can do it
Pre-contemplation	Not thinking about it
Contemplation	Thinking about it

Technical/jargon word	Everyday way of saying it

continued

F3.1   continued...

Technical/jargon word	Everyday way of saying it

Facilitator's Worksheet F3.2: Responding to Diverse Needs

Use the chart below to identify your current strengths when responding to the diverse needs of the individuals you work with.

Note how you might usefully develop your skills.

Diversity issue	Existing strengths and resources 'I already use...'	Tips for development
Example Working with a service user with dyslexia	• 12 plus font plus • Arial or comic sans • Short sentences • Bullet points	• Find out what this individual has found most helpful • Avoid abbreviations • Use **bold** rather than <u>underlining</u> • Find out and use preferred coloured paper if relevant

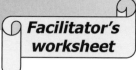

Facilitator's Worksheet
F3.3: Reflective Practice

1. Describe the needs of two very different service users.

2. How will you adapt your practice and materials used to meet their needs?
By...I will
....
....
....
....
....

3. When you have tried the methods and materials, describe what went well:

4. And what went less well:

5. What have you learnt from the experience?

6. What will you do differently next time?

SUMMARY

A motivational approach is essentially responsive to the individual you are working with.

'One size does not fit all.'

The first part of this chapter looks at how rapport between two people is essential for good communication. The second part focuses on making a clear contract that brings purpose to the communication. *Without rapport there can be no influence.*

You can establish rapport with a person which allows dialogue and builds respect without having to agree with their choices. Many people do this unconsciously, but there are specific skills which can enhance rapport. You may already use many of them, but it is worth becoming aware of what they are and then you can work to enhance those that improve rapport in different situations.

The message for practitioners, as well as for service users is, 'increase your choices by increasing your repertoire of behaviours'.

You instinctively know when you are in rapport with someone else. You might describe yourself to be:

- In touch with
- Seeing eye to eye
- Tuned into each other

Without rapport, communication is clumsy and full of misunderstanding.

You will know you can establish rapport with some people more quickly and easily than with others. For some you have to work extremely hard to develop any rapport. You will have a range of skills available to you, but some service users may have very few people skills. Others may be particularly good at developing rapport with some types of people, but may not have a full range of skills in their repertoire. The responsibility to develop rapport is first and foremost with the facilitator. The responsibility to make choices is with the service user.

Many of the ideas below come originally from Neuro-Lingusitic Programming/NLP (Laborde 1987), which offers clear explanations of what happens in interactions and teaches how we can consciously learn to adopt useful behaviours.

THE KNOWLEDGE AND SKILLS FOR RAPPORT

1. Valuing the person, if not the behaviour
2. Understanding rapport as a process
3. The communication cycle
4. Using appropriate matching behaviours
5. Understanding the dance of rapport
6. How to read and use body language (see Chapter 7)
7. High level listening skills (see Chapter 7)
8. How to reflect back key themes (see Chapter 8).

Valuing the Person, if not the Behaviour

Your own skills may not be enough. Rapport can be lost long before you meet the person you will work with. The initial referral, if less than courteous and clear, can set up resistance, which may then be compounded by a poor reception when they visit your agency. You may well have experienced your own anxiety turning to anger as bureaucracy and discourtesy come between you and the service you are seeking. Valuing the person starts with the first contact and is expressed in the way every part of the agency approaches service users. When you visit an institution, you know by the time you have passed through reception, whether this is an institution of respect, or one that demeans all who enter therein.

Understanding Rapport as a Process

- The degree of rapport will vary according to the reason you are together and how well you can communicate.
- Different degrees of rapport are appropriate to different situations.
- Within any interchange, you can expect the level of rapport to go up and down.
- When rapport is lost, the skill is to focus on building rapport (by listening, by reflecting and body language) not ploughing on with the agenda.

The Communication Cycle

Before you look in detail at how rapport works, it might be helpful to consider the processes that occur when two people communicate.

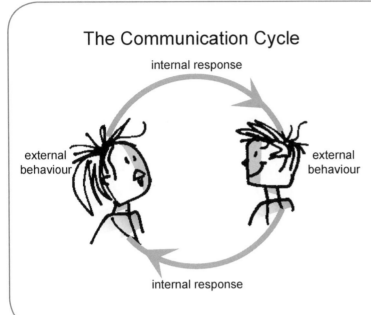

The Communication Cycle

internal response

external behaviour

external behaviour

internal response

1. Avril 'behaves' (perhaps turns her head towards Bill).
2. When her behaviour is noticed by Bill, he develops an internal response in his head (picture, thought, etc.).
3. This internal response results in Bill making a new external response (perhaps he smiles), which is in turn experienced by Avril.
4. She then has an internal response and makes a new external response (perhaps she waves her hand) ... which is seen by Bill ... and so on ...

A few kinds of external behaviours and internal responses are listed here by way of illustration.

Internal response	**External behaviours**
Thoughts, emotions, pictures, words, sounds, expectations, memories, feelings.	Posture, gestures, face, eyes, voice, touch, clothing, skin tone.

You can get a clue to what your behaviour means to the other person from the response you get. This may or may not be what you intended.

It is relatively easy to blame the other person if the interaction is not successful. Much depends on the interpretation of your behaviour by the other person. Only by checking out can you discover how the other person read your behaviour.

Perhaps the simple communication above goes differently. Avril may think, 'Why is he grinning at me and trying to chat me up?' And this translates into different behaviour, she turns her back on Bill.

The meaning of your communication is the response you get

Which may be different to the one you intended!

You cannot know how your well-intentioned communication may be received by someone else, unless you accurately observe the response you get.

The Facilitator's response ability
You cannot change others, but … you can change your behaviour to get a different response.

The facilitator's response ability

As the worker it is your responsibility to listen with your eyes and ears so that you will know when the response you get is different to that which you intended. When this happens, *it is important information about the effect of your behaviour.* You can then either change your behaviour or explore what this was about and learn more from the person you are working with. In doing the latter, you are of course also changing your behaviour. If you persist in your original behaviour (sometimes more forcefully), you are likely to get the same or an even stronger similar response. It is all too easy to then label the other person with that response. Then you are both stuck.

Being aware of the interpretation that the other person has reached enables you to try different behaviours and tactics; to communicate the meaning you did intend. This approach empowers those who have a repertoire of behaviours they can try. But it also preserves the integrity of the other person who remains in control of, and responsible for, their own responses. If what you are doing is not working as you intended, try something different. This book will offer you lots of different skills and strategies to try.

> If what you are doing is not working,
> do something different.

Using Appropriate Matching Behaviours

The first stages of rapport are linked to matching. This is not the same as trying to copycat or ape someone else. Rapport occurs naturally but we can increase our rapport skills by paying attention to matching. Often only one or two areas are matched initially, perhaps posture and rhythms.

Handshaking is a good example of both.

Here are some examples of matching:

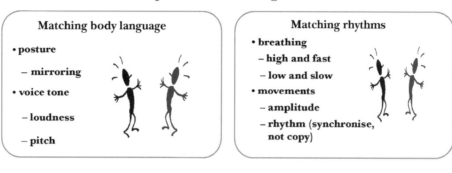

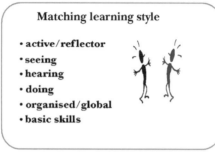

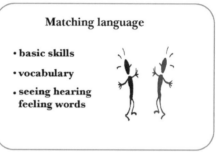

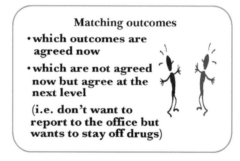

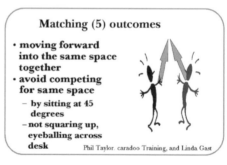

Source: reproduced by permission of Phil Taylor and Linda Gast.

Simple matching behaviours

Matching behaviours can enhance rapport. At a simple level, this may mean you adopting a similar posture to the person you are paying close attention to. Often this happens naturally. However, in more complex exchanges, you may not want to match and reinforce all that is being described. For instance, you would not wish to match the angry posture of an annoyed client.

For a fight to take place, two people need to match behaviours. A glance at any conflict on television will show the protagonists have remarkably matched behaviours. If one of them adopted a completely different behaviour it would be difficult for the conflict to continue. Imagine if, in the middle of a boxing match, one of them sits down and starts writing a note to the other! So matching all behaviours tends to reinforce both mood and the activity.

Matching rhythms

For workers it seems the crucial skill is to match natural rhythms, so that you are literally in harmony with the other's body language. Experiment with an understanding friend, try deliberately setting up a disharmonious rhythm and see the conversation falter, or even anger develop.

Often our concern to follow our agenda as advisor or helper will establish a rhythm in our own body language, which unconsciously fights the rhythm of the person trying to get our understanding.

Matching outcomes

Another important 'matching' is that of matching outcomes. What do you both want? At first your agendas may seem incompatible, but at some level you may both want the same thing. You may, for instance, both want the service user to have a better life.

Exploring long-term outcomes is at the heart of motivational skills and the way in which this is achieved without manipulating those you help is described in the following pages. If you do manipulate or use power to get them to agree with you, chances are they will go away and do their own thing anyway.

A clear open understanding of why and how you meet is also important, and this is discussed below, in the section on contracts.

Matching, pacing and leading

You can match to establish rapport and then gradually lead the person to a different and more useful state for the work in hand. If someone is angry you might match the energy of the person with the intensity of your listening. A straight physical matching would of course feed the mood, which would become exaggerated, in other words, more angry, more depressed. This is what football hooligans do when they get out of control together, each matching the others' behaviour and adding to an increasing violence.

Equally you can lead people to a state where they can reflect and learn. In a tense situation at first you might match the energy, perhaps by listening intently with a non-threatening posture. Then by gradually relaxing your posture, whilst maintaining rapport, the service user can be lead to a more relaxed state in which the difficulty can be explored.

Reflective listening, empathy, open questions and affirming all contribute to increasing rapport and helping the service user to access that part of themselves that can explore their difficulties in a useful way. This may take a time or even some sessions, but first rapport is established, and then there is a gradual leading to a new state.

Your responses may be thoughtful and strategic, but if they are not genuine, it will show in your natural rhythms and body language, and rapport will be diminished. Your skilful responses and body language can offer space and opportunity for the other to respond to you in a way that enables them to unlock their own resources.

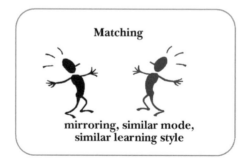

Matching

mirroring, similar mode, similar learning style

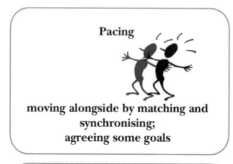

Pacing

moving alongside by matching and synchronising; agreeing some goals

Leading

leading gradually to a new state

Which leads to

a new rapport for work on stuck behaviour

Understanding the Dance of Rapport

The degree of rapport needs to be appropriate to the occasion. In any encounter, the degree of rapport changes back and forth as the encounter proceeds.

Rapport is like a dance in which the partners move constantly, each responding to the other, sometimes you pace the other; sometimes you may lead the other.

You normally begin an encounter with a lower level of rapport and the rapport then increases to a level appropriate to the occasion. In counselling or friendship the 'working level' of rapport can be very high.

Equally important you reduce rapport in the closing stages so that you can part without either party being 'left up in the air'.

In reality, especially when working in difficult areas, rapport is sometimes lost in the middle of an interview. As you become aware of the loss, it helps to focus your attention on building rapport, rather than ploughing on with the content.

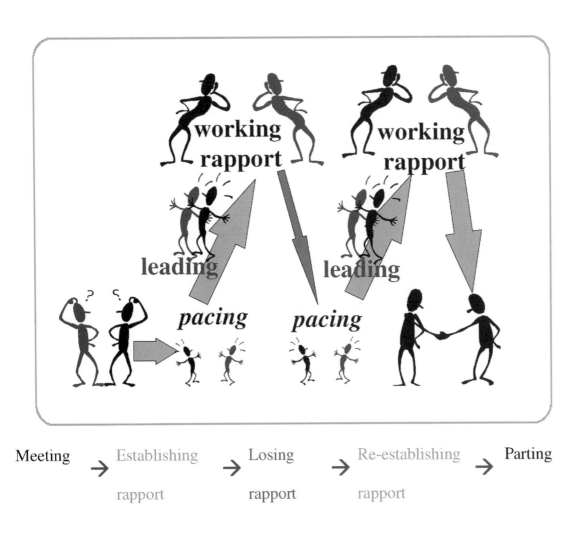

| Meeting | → | Establishing rapport | → | Losing rapport | → | Re-establishing rapport | → | Parting |

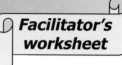

Facilitator's Worksheet F4.1: The Optimum Conditions for Rapport.

Consider how and where you meet with service users and check out the following. Note highs and lows and what might be done differently.

Action	Works against rapport	Promotes rapport
Initial referral		
Letters and appointments		
Reception		
Room furniture, decorations, posters, etc.		
Room layout (over a desk or side by side)		
Time available		
Distractions for the facilitator		
Clear contract		
Pressure for the facilitator to achieve a result (your agenda)		
Awareness of service user's responses		
Proportion of session in which the facilitator was listening		
Use of reflections and open questions		
Matching, pacing and leading skills		
Closing the session		
Arrangements for next appointment		
Any other factors		

Facilitator's Worksheet F4.2: Matching, Pacing, Leading

The purpose of this exercise is to become more aware of the way in which your behaviour can impact on the behaviour of others. Note the behaviours that seem to promote good conditions, when working with the concerns of both your agency and the service user.

The exercise

Make opportunity to observe the following kinds of interaction. They may take place in your agency, or in your everyday life. You may need to ask permission of those you observe and agree to share your findings with them. You might set this up as part of a training exercise. Where possible check out what you observed with their experience.

Note what you can see and hear that seems to inhibit or promotes rapport when:

1. Two people greet each other
2. Two people seem to be transacting some business successfully
3. Two people are apparently in disagreement, or at loggerheads with each other
4. Over a period in time, one person seems to lead the other to a more useful state for the business in hand.

Use the check list below to help your observation.

Some observation pointers

- Body postures – mirroring?
- Harmony of natural rhythms? (Speech, hand movements, breathing, head, eyes, feet, etc.)
- Energy matching? (Intensity of listening, behaviour)
- Voice? (Pitch, rhythm, speed, volume, tone)
- Eyes? (Contact, movements, gestures)
- Amplitude of gestures and movements? (Small contained movements or large expansive gestures, fast or slow)
- Congruity between what is said and non-verbal behaviour?
- What response is each apparently giving to the other?
- Is the response most apparent from the body? hands? face?

Facilitator's Worksheet F4.3: The Power of Influence

The exercise

This exercise is for the brave with a willing partner or preferably a small group.

One person agrees to tell a short story from their life that they think the listener would like to hear. When the story starts, the listener, unknown to the story teller, tries to inhibit the story teller by using subtle, non-verbal behaviour. The listener might try mismatching, or set up a small rhythm in their foot or hand that is disharmonious with the rhythm of the story teller. The other members of the group observe. After five minutes or so stop and ask the story teller what their experience was. Then take the observations from the group.

The learning

Often the story teller will realise what is happening, but no matter, their story will still be inhibited in some way. Some can no longer tell a coherent story, or cut it short. Some even say it was not a very good story anyway. The lesson, which is sobering, is that even when you know it is just an exercise, your ability to tell a story can be seriously affected by the response of others. Some even take responsibility for the 'poor story' when it was entirely the result of the listeners' deliberate behaviour. How much more, therefore, can your behaviour disable or enable those you work with.

MAKING A CLEAR CONTRACT

Good rapport is not itself a sufficient mandate for work between two people. What gives the work integrity is a contract that is understood and agreed by all concerned. The contract itself depends on a clear understanding of the authority, rights and purpose that underpins any particular piece of work.

Motivational work has a purpose.

First purpose

- **Seeks to develop *motivation* to change**
- **to something desirable for the agency and the community as well as the service user**

Although a motivational approach draws heavily on the work of Carl Rogers (1959) it is not totally client centred. *The facilitator has a clear purpose*, which may or may not be shared at the start by the service user. The facilitator is trying to generate motivation for change in a direction, which is seen to be more socially desirable or healthier for both the service user and the community. The facilitator may work for an agency that has explicit purposes. The integrity of the facilitator in working to this purpose is intact if the service user understands that this is the reason behind the service that is being offered.

You cannot, however, impose long-term change on someone, such change comes from within. The *second purpose* of a motivational approach, therefore, is to help the service user to do the change work, and to take responsibility for the things they are saying about themselves including any inherent discrepancy between behaviour and goals.

Second purpose

Help them draw a self-portrait, complete with inconsistencies and contrasts

A clear contract will recognise the concerns, rights and responsibilities of each person. Chapter 1 suggests you start by thinking about what you call your service users. 'Patient'; 'friend'; 'service user'; 'offender'; 'student'; 'colleague', all imply a different kinds of contract, with different expectations and boundaries.

Each agency or professional body will have their own expectations of the worker and the 'client'.

Visiting an advice agency may be completely voluntary. Even so, the advice workers will have codes of practice, and certain behaviours from the clients would not be acceptable. Exactly what can and cannot be offered, payment or free, and any promise of confidentiality would all be part of contract.

An offender meeting a criminal justice worker under a court order will be in a very different position. The court will have defined what is required of both and there are specific legal sanctions if these are not met. The interests of the offender will be secondary to public safety.

Education and Health workers might have a professional relationship anywhere between these two, depending on their role and where they work.

See Trotter (1999) if you want to explore the tensions of contracting with 'involuntary clients' further.

Authority, Purpose and Freedom

Motivational skills can be used in all these situations, as the approach assumes the worker will have an agenda, which may not be the same as those they are working with. What is crucial is making clear at the start exactly what each can expect of the other and what constraints, resources and sanctions are available. The motivational approach has the worker as facilitator helping the person they work with to evaluate and commit to change for themselves. The service user is always free to decide either way. The facilitator will help them include the consequences in the balance and be clear as to what will happen if they decide not to change, or to change in a way unacceptable to the agency or the law. But this is information, given without judgement. Whilst the facilitator will make it clear in the contract they can only support action for change in certain directions, they will make it equally clear that the service user is free to decide at all times.

What is in the Contract?

If you are employed, your agency may already have guide lines for your work. The following open questions may help you establish what should be in the contract between you and the service user.

1. What does the agency require of me in this piece of work?
2. What does my professional body require of me?
3. What can the service user expect of me?
4. What can I expect of the service user?
5. What fees or payments are required?
6. What external constraints or resources apply?
7. What will you aim to achieve together?
8. How, where and when will you meet?

After establishing rapport it is important to clarify boundaries and expectations. In an interview situation, this might be a structured statement clarifying the purpose of the work. It might also include a written statement. Even at this stage, motivational skills are crucial. Open questions and reflections will help check out understanding of the structured statement and negotiate any changes. The aim is to produce self-motivating statements from the service user about the contract. In this way some genuine agreement about the nature and scope of the work you can do together can be established. In some situations the contract may need to be reviewed frequently.

SUMMARY

This chapter has explored a little of the mechanisms that underpin human communication, particularly how each person influences the other. The knowledge may help you build rapport. Rapport is not enough. For influence to have integrity there needs to be a clear agreed contract between the parties.

Both rapport and contracts are likely to change and require constant attention, throughout any piece of work.

The next chapters look in detail at the communication skills vital to a motivational approach.

> 'Seek first to understand and then to be understood.'

You cannot put motivation in a wheelbarrow! You cannot give it to another person or force someone to have it, although we often talk as though you could. We also talk about it as though it were a fixed thing, rather than something that is constantly changing. When you talk about motivation as a thing, it becomes more fixed and difficult to change. You can easily forget that motivation is a process.

Motivation is about the goals you choose from moment to moment, including choosing to do nothing.

Compare:

You need to get him motivated. *[It's your job to motivate him!]*

with

This morning she was unwilling to get out of bed and go to her appointment. *[Her responsibility, her thinking, her behaviour]*

Motivation for change is, therefore, more than compliance; it is more than agreement with the facilitator or complying to avoid a threat. You are truly motivated for change if you have the *conviction* to change, the *confidence* to change and the *commitment* to change now. You are motivated to change when you hear yourself say:

'I want to change'

'I can change'

'I will change, now'

(*Adapted from Miller and Rollnick 2002*)

Components of motivation	Signs of low motivation *Resistance talk*	High motivation *Self-motivating statements/change talk*
'I want to' Conviction 	'I don't give a xxxx.' 'Why should I…' 'Ah but….'	'I want to change because…' 'It is important for me to change.' 'I' m concerned about my present behaviour.' 'The good things about changing are…'
'I can' Confidence 	'I can't.' 'It's not my fault.' 'They need to change, not me.' 'It's outside my control.'	'I can do this.' 'I have these skills.' 'I did it before.' 'I will be able to do it in these situations.' 'If that happens I will do this…'

'I will change' *Commitment*	'I won't.' 'I might change sometime.' 'Not now.'	'Now's the right time.' 'I will make the first step.' 'I've started.' 'This is how I will do it.'

Setting Goals for Change

Where conviction, confidence and commitment to change are high, initiating talk about change can be straightforward. In response to a referral the facilitator need only welcome the service user and after an opening statement, ask for the service user's views on what they want to change.

For example:

> *Facilitator:* **I understand that you have asked to see me in order to develop a plan to reduce your alcohol intake.**
>
> *Service User:* Yes, that's right I would like to cut down my drinking so that I can get my driving licence back and I am concerned about the effect it is having on my health and my work.

Where the service user is less willing, able or not yet ready to consider change, this approach may lead to immediate resistance.

> *Facilitator:* **I understand that you have asked to see me in order to develop a plan to reduce your alcohol intake.**
>
> *Service user:* Yes, but, I'm not an alcoholic, I haven't got a problem with drinking.

A direct question such as that given below can exacerbate the reaction further:

> *Facilitator:* **Don't you think you should be controlling your drinking more?**

Where conviction, confidence or commitment is low, it can be helpful to take a step back and explore what the service user is currently motivated to do and then seek a shared agenda for you both to work on.

The authors of this Toolkit worked within a criminal justice agency concerned with reducing offending. Initially, many of the service users did not share this goal. They gained a great deal of short-term benefit from some of their offences and at first, seemed stuck in this pattern. Many, however, did change because they discovered their own reasons to do so.

In the example below, Jake is very motivated to take heroin; he wants to experience the effects of taking it, he has the skills to obtain and use heroin and he is willing to go to great efforts to obtain it. He also has the potential to use this energy and skill in a different direction, if he can find a reason to change. Jake has given clues to what these reasons may be. He has hinted that he does not feel able to cope with prison, he wants a job, he does not much like stealing or selling heroin. At this point, Jake is saying it is all outside of his control and responds with an 'ah but' to all suggestions. The Toolkit will help you work with service users like Jake and draw out positive values, such as a desire to be more honest, compassionate or to improve themselves, which conflict with the path they are starting to take. It is this internal conflict that can provide self-motivation for change. The facilitator's worksheet F5.1 below can help you assess current motivation and identify any goals which may be shared at this stage.

'People are usually more convinced by reasons they discover themselves than by those found by others.'

Blaise Pascal 1623

Jake's current motivation

'I can, but I don't want to' Sell heroin and steal.	**'I want to, I can, I will'** Take smack (heroin)
Cope with going to prison **'I can't and I don't want to'**	Get a job **'I want to but I can't'**

Service user's worksheet

Service User's Worksheet S5.1:

Discuss the worksheet with your facilitator and then fill in the boxes below.

'I can, but I don't want to'	**'I want to, I can, I will'**
'I can't and I don't want to'	**'I want to but I can't'**

Facilitator's Worksheet
F5.1: Finding Shared Goals

Discuss exercise S5.1 above with the service user.

Listen for and identify areas of overlap between:

The service user's goals..

Your goals ....

Where there is overlap there is potential for working together towards change.

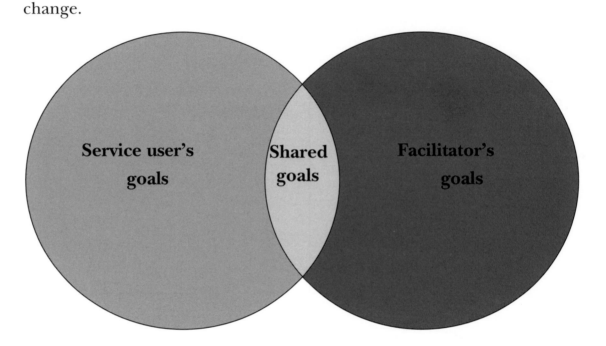

SUMMARY

Motivation is not a fixed state and it can not be given to someone. The degree of motivation an individual has for a particular goal or outcome will fluctuate, depending on their desires and circumstances. The motivational facilitator helps the service user clarify the direction for change by gaining rapport, responding to what the service user currently wants and feels able to do and gently helping them towards a shared desired outcome. Change occurs, when the individual can honestly say, 'I want to, I can and I will change.'

The next chapter explores the stages people tend to go through when making changes, and the skills that are most helpful at each stage.

Chapter

6

Chapter 5 explored how a motivational approach challenges the notion that some people are motivated to change and others are not; that the former can be effectively changed, whilst the latter cannot. Everyone can be open to change. Motivation to change is not fixed: it is an internal process that fluctuates over time. Motivation is measured by the extent someone may *want* to change, feels they *can* change and decides they *will change* now. Prochaska and Di Clemente's (1982) *'cycle of change'* provides a useful model for exploring how degrees of motivation develop into stages of change. The model suggests tasks that typically need to be achieved within each stage, in order to move on to the next stage. Sometimes these tasks are achieved without the help of someone else. The service users you are working with may be stuck at one of the earlier stages and a motivational approach can help them to move on.

A more detailed analysis of the theory and evidence base of the cycle of change can be found in Chapter 1. Chapter 6 provides:

- A summary of the cycle of change to use in everyday work
- Exercises to help service users understand their current stage of motivation to change
- Exercises to help you identify relevant skills to use at each stage of change.

The chapters that follow will explore in more depth how to apply the skills within the spirit of a motivational approach.

WHAT IS THE CYCLE OF CHANGE?

The chances are that you have experienced the cycle of change yourself. Think back to a time when you changed a pattern of behaviour. How would you describe the stages which led up to you deciding to change? Examples people have shared in training courses have included: deciding to stop smoking, changing a diet, cutting back on drinking, establishing an exercise routine or driving within speed limits.

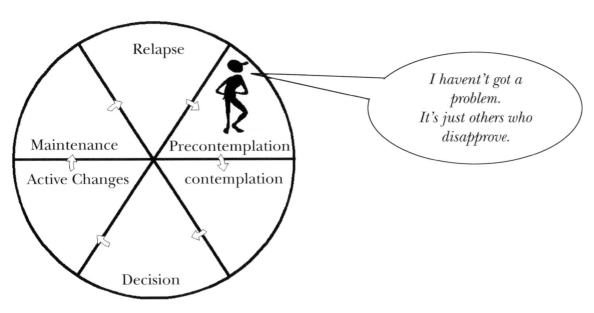

At the initial stage of change you may not be aware that there is a problem. You could be gradually putting on weight, or driving over the speed limit, or not taking prescribed drugs. You either don't notice or don't care. If you think about your behaviour at all you might be saying to yourself: *'I don't need to change.'* You may feel angry if others tried to persuade you to change. You have yet to contemplate any change.

You are at the *pre-contemplation stage.*

In order to move onto the *contemplation stage* you become aware that your behaviour is linked with an outcome you do not want. For instance, you cannot get into your usual clothes; you receive a speeding ticket, or you start to feel ill.

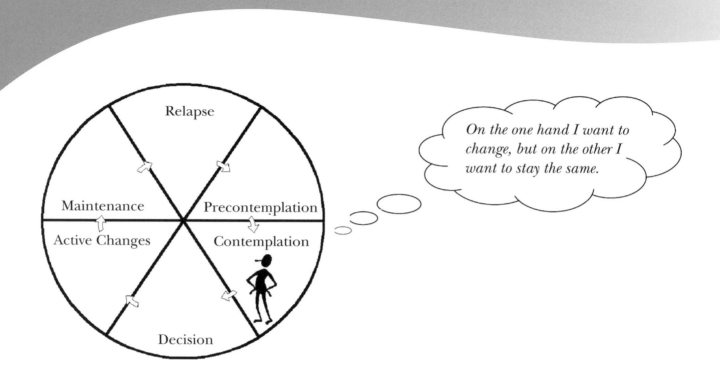

This is the stage where you start to be uncomfortable with your behaviour. You struggle with the thought *'Do I want to change or not?'* *'Can I change even if I wanted to?'* You can see both the advantages and disadvantages of change. At times you think you will change and might even make a small step to do so, but the next day you return to your previous behaviour. You may feel confused and uncertain. You are in the *contemplation stage.*

You begin to move towards the *decision stage* when your reasons to change become greater than your reasons to stay the same. You may realise that your reasons to change are linked with longer term values. You are starting to identify how to overcome the barriers and feel confident that you can make a start.

At the *decision stage* you make a clear decision to change your behaviour. You may feel happy and focused, or you may feel anxious. You might say to yourself:

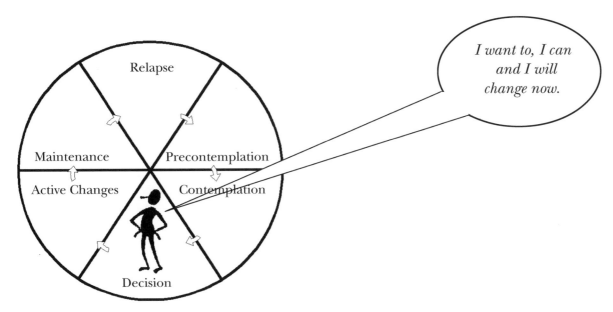

To move onto the *action stage* you plan what you are going to do. You might well remember when you thought you had made a clear decision previously. Somehow the plans you made never materialised. Deep down you were still at the contemplation stage.

At the *action stage* you start to change your behaviour. You may still be aware of your previous behaviour and experience a tendency to revert to you old ways.

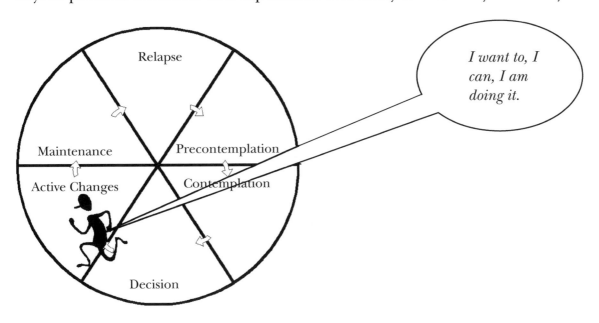

Gradually, or sometimes suddenly, you like your new behaviours and are clear that you really do want this change. You develop the skills and confidence to maintain your new chosen behaviour and overcome the day-to-day temptations to return to your previous behaviour.

A slip or *lapse* is common when changing behaviour and on average occurs about seven times before change occurs. You may therefore have a lapse. For a period of time you return to your previous behaviour.

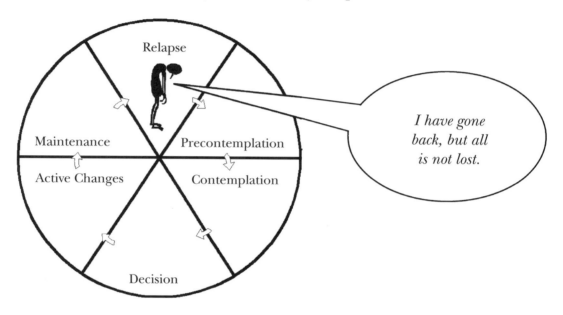

In order to rejoin the cycle you treat this as an opportunity to learn from your experience. You return to *contemplation*, however briefly, and remind yourself of the main reasons you want to change and reassure yourself that you can change.

At the *maintenance stage* you keep the change going; the changed behaviour will start to become a part of your life. You can say to yourself

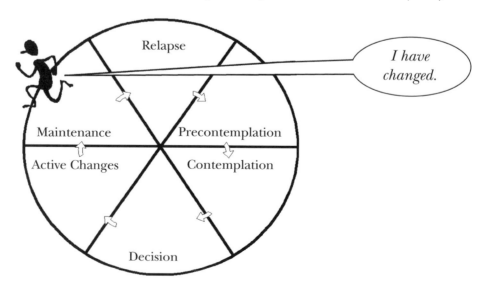

When the new behaviour is integrated into your lifestyle and you no longer need to remind yourself of the reasons to maintain the behaviour, you can be said to have left the cycle completely.

A motivational approach has been found to be particularly effective in the early stages of change when someone is uncertain if they *want* to change (the *pre-contemplation* and *contemplation* stages of change). At the *decision* stage, when someone wants to change, but still needs to develop the confidence to feel they can, the integration of a motivational approach with information giving and skills development works well. When a *lapse* occurs, a return to a motivational approach is again useful.

The exercises that follow are designed to be used alongside an interview to explore the stages of motivation. The exercises will need the use of skills in *reflective listening, open questions* and *affirmation*. These skills are explored in depth in the subsequent chapters and you may find it helpful to return to these exercises once you have read those chapters.

Some service users will respond better to a discussion based on the ideas within these exercises: everyone you work with is different. In using and adapting the exercises it is helpful to consider learning styles, culture, gender, age, disability, ability, sexuality, religion and race. (See Chapter 3 for further information about learning styles.)

Stages of change can be in constant fluctuation. Service users may be at a particular stage of change for one behaviour, whilst at quite another stage for a different behaviour. For example, someone who has been diagnosed as HIV positive may be at the *pre-contemplation* stage about not sharing needles, but be *contemplating* using condoms. Even within one interview the stage of change may alter. You and the service users are likely to overestimate desire and confidence to change. It is usually safe to assume that the lowest level of stage indicated is the more accurate.

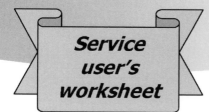

Service User's Worksheet S6.1: Self-assessment of Motivation to Change

1. Tick the statements which apply to you
2. Add comments on the dotted lines.
3. Write or draw your feelings.

What behaviour are you considering changing/keeping?

....

Stage of change

What you say to others

Pre-contemplation

☐ Others believe I need to change. I do not see it as a problem.

☐ I have not thought about changing the behaviour before.

☐ I feel annoyed and angry that others want to change me.

☐ I think/feel that change is hopeless.

☐ I can see many more reasons to stay the same rather than change.

♦ I feel ....

I haven't got a problem. It's just others who disapprove.

I want to carry on most because
....
....
....

S6.1 continued...

Contemplation

- ☐ I have doubts about my lifestyle
- ☐ I am weighing up the pros and cons of change
- ☐ I want to change but am unsure if I can
- ☐ I want to but I don't know if I can
- ☐ I would like to change, but now is not the right time
- ♦ I feel.................................

On the one hand I want to change because ....

....

....

but on the other hand I don't want to change because

....

....

Decision

- ☐ I am ready to make choices to change
- ☐ Change fits with my long-term goals and values
- ☐ I believe I can make a start
- ☐ I believe I will change
- ☐ Now is the right time to start
- ♦ I feel.................................

- ♦ How much do I want to change?
  0.................................10
  Not at all   Very much

- ♦ How confident am I that I will
  0.................................10
  I won't   I will

I want to change because.................................

....

I can change because.................................

....

I will start

....

....

By.....................I will have

- ♦ ....
  ....
  ....
- ♦ ....
  ....
  ....

S6.1 continued...

Action
- ☐ I am taking steps to actively change my behaviour
- ☐ I want to change
- ☐ I believe I can change
- ☐ Now is the right time
- ♦ I feel...............................

> I have started
>
> to...
> ....
> ....
> ....

Maintenance
- ☐ I have changed my behaviour for 6 months or more
- ☐ I am developing new skills to overcome any barriers to change
- ☐ I am happy with the change and want to continue
- ♦ I feel...............................

> I am most at risk of returning to my previous behaviour when..
> ....
> ....
> If this happens I will...................
> ....

> I am changing.

> I have gone back but all is not lost.

Relapse or lapse
- ☐ I have returned to a pattern of behaviour linked to problem areas
- ☐ This is a one-off
- ☐ This is more than a one-off.
- ☐ I feel reluctant to start again
- ☐ I want learn from the experience
- ♦ I feel...............................

> I have learnt that
> ....
> ....
> ....
> ....

S6.1   continued...

Return to the cycle

- ☐ I am learning from the lapse
- ☐ I want to change
- ☐ I can change
- ☐ I will change
- ♦ I feel................................

I have learnt from the lapse.

Exit from the cycle

- ☐ I have changed my behaviour
- ☐ I have learnt new behaviours
- ☐ I have new life
- ♦ I feel................................

I have changed.

Service User's Worksheet S6.2: Where am I on the Cycle of Change?

Identify which stages most apply to your behaviour and discuss the reasons with your key worker.

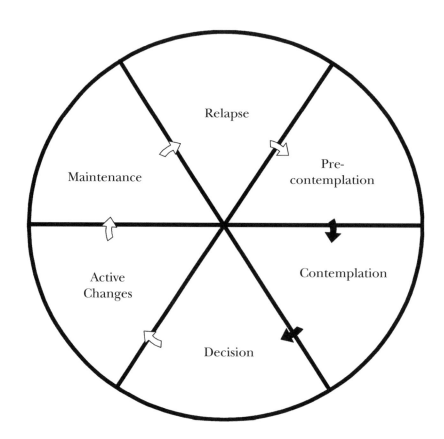

Service User's Worksheet S6.3: Alternative Cycle of Change

Use this worksheet instead of worksheet 6.2 if you find it more helpful.

Identify which areas of the cycle are most relevant to your behaviour and discuss with your key worker.

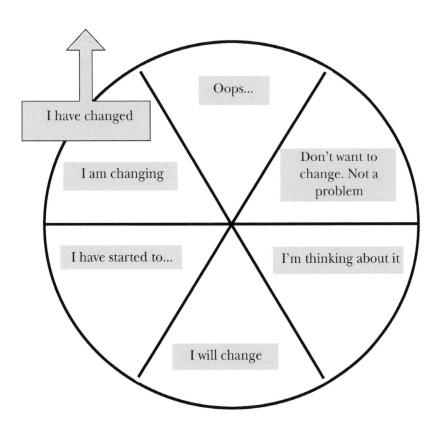

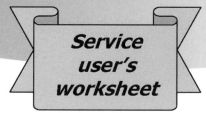

Service User's Worksheet S64: Exploring Change - Thoughts, Feelings and Behaviour

Use this self-help worksheet to think back on how you changed a pattern of behaviour in the past.

I don't want to change – *Pre-contemplation*		
What did I do?	**What did I think?**	**How did I feel?** (Draw or write)

Thinking about it. – *Contemplation*		
What did I do?	**What did I think?**	**How did I feel?**

S6.4   continued...

Decision		
What did I do?	**What did I think?**	**How did I feel?**

Action		
What did I do?	**What did I think?**	**How did I feel?**

S6.4   continued...

I changed – *Maintenance*		
What did I do?	**What did I think?**	**How did I feel?**

I slipped back – *Lapse*		
What did I do?	**What did I think?**	**How did I feel?**

S64   continued...

Return to cycle		
What did I do?	**What did I think?**	**How did I feel?**

Exit from cycle **Changed behaviour long term**		
What did I do?	**What did I think?**	**How did I feel?**

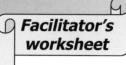

Facilitator's Worksheet F6.1: Possible Answers to Service User's Worksheet S6.1

Typical reactions are recorded below. The answers can be clues to where someone is on the cycle of change. We would however, suggest caution as these are only indicators. Where you are on the cycle can fluctuate even within the same interview.

I don't want to – *Pre-contemplation*		
What did I do?	**What did I think?**	**How did I feel?**
Carried on as before.	I haven't even thought about changing. Everyone tries to control me. I won't change. I don't want to change. There are lots of reasons to stay as I am. I can't change, there is no point in thinking about it.	Content with behaviour, reluctant to change. Angry with those who suggest change. Rebellious. Confident and determined to stay the same. Calm, rationalising Resigned, depressed.

F6.1   continued...

Thinking about it–*Contemplation*		
What did I do?	**What did I think?**	**How did I feel?**
Carried on as before	I want to and I don't want to. This isn't working, but I know where I am and feel safe. I am not sure if I can. I'll start sometime.	Confused Dissatisfied Depressed Stuck May be angry when advised.

Decision		
What did I do?	**What did I think?**	**How did I feel?**
Made an action plan. I Just got on and did it. I told someone else I was giving up.	I am going to change. I want to, but not sure if I can, but I will try. I will miss the buzz.	Optimistic Purposeful Some anxiety Excited

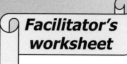

F6.1   continued...

Action		
What did I do?	**What did I think?**	**How did I feel?**
Started changing behaviour	This is going well I can do it I need to keep to targets. Can I keep it up?	Good Proud Excited some anxiety Tempted to return to previous behaviour

Maintenance		
What did I do?	**What did I think?**	**How did I feel?**
Continued changing for several months.	This is going well. Perhaps I don't need to worry about it anymore. What'll happen if....	Relaxed Good Complacent May be some anxiety

F6.1   continued...

Lapse		
What did I do?	**What did I think?**	**How did I feel?**
Returned to previous behaviour.	I cant do this after all. Is it worth trying to change? It wasn't my fault. Perhaps I could try again.	Deflated Let down Angry Guilty Sad Renewed determination.

Return to cycle		
What did I do?	**What did I think?**	**How did I feel?**
Identified how the lapse occurred and planned what to do next time. Went around the cycle again.	I want to change because... I am likely to be tempted to return to my previous behaviour when... If it happens again I will... I have learnt	Anxious Guilty Angry Optimistic Determined

F6.1 continued...

Exit from cycle Changed behaviour		
What did I do?	**What did I think?**	**How did I feel?**
New behaviour became part of my life.	I have managed to do it. If I can change this I can change other things. Focus on new behaviour and new life.	Proud Happy Successful Optimistic

Facilitator's Worksheet F6.2: Enhancing empathy and assessing stages of motivation

This worksheet has been designed to help you make a provisional assessment of the stage(s) of motivation which are most relevant to your service user. Answer the questions below with reference to the discussions you have had with the service user. You may find it helpful to copy the sheet, date it and revisit it at a later stage.

What specifically is the behaviour that is causing the service user problems? Indicate on the cycle of change which stage(s) of change you think is most relevant to the service user now.

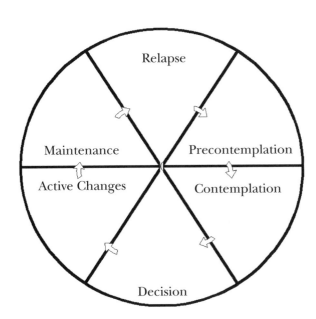

What is the evidence for your judgement?

What does the service user do and say?

What do you think their thoughts about the behaviour are?

How do you think they feel?

What response from you do you think the service user will find most helpful?

Facilitator's Worksheet F6.3-1:
Responding to Different Stages of Change

Identify which skills you, as a facilitator, are using at which stage.

Pre-contemplation

DESIRED OUTCOMES
Raise doubt
Problem recognition

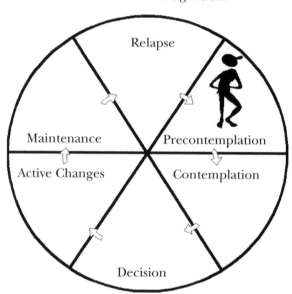

Most useful strategies
☐ Create rapport
☐ Reflective listening
☐ Gain empathy
If reluctant to change also
☐ Provide new information/feedback.
If rebellious
☐ Listen to resistance
☐ Emphasise choice
If resigned to not changing
☐ Believe in change and explore strengths.
If giving reasons not to change
☐ Explore reasons not to change then any reasons to change
☐ Explore wider goals and how they fit in with your agency goals.

Least useful
☐ Try to talk people into change
☐ Argue them into discomfort
☐ Make a judgement about their behaviour
☐ Use authority to insist upon change
☐ Provide advice, especially if pre-contemplation is rebellious or rationalising

Self assessment

Facilitator's Worksheet F6.3-2: Contemplation

DESIRED OUTCOMES

Concern with present behaviour

Desire to change

Confidence to make a start

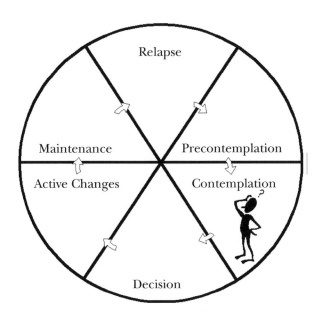

Most useful strategies

☐ Explore the reasons not to change as well as the reasons to change - ambivalence

☐ Explore the problem

☐ What are the most important things in their lives?

☐ Reflect the gap/ discrepancy between long-term goals and present behaviour

☐ Explore confidence to change

☐ Identify barriers to change and strengths to overcome these

☐ Reflect back statements of desire and confidence to start

Least useful

☐ Give advice

☐ Attempt to solve problems (e.g. have you thought about doing...?)

☐ Bring in your own experience (when I was...)

☐ Ask closed questions

☐ Work only with the positives for changing and ignore the negatives

☐ Try to teach new skills before there is a desire to change

Self assessment

Facilitator's Worksheet F6.3-3:
Decision Stage

DESIRED OUTCOME
Optimism about change
Action plan

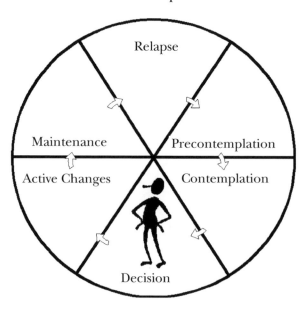

Most useful strategies

- ☐ Check there are both verbal and non verbal expressions of desire to change.(Congruence)
- ☐ Explore confidence to change
- ☐ Clarify joint goals
- ☐ Explore options to achieve goals
- ☐ Explore consequences of options
- ☐ Select an option
- ☐ Identify small steps
- ☐ Identify barriers and how to overcome
- ☐ Identify who will help
- ☐ Plan to monitor and reward success.
- ☐ Visualise success

Least useful

- ☐ Rush to action
- ☐ Assume ambivalence is gone
- ☐ Work for solutions too early
- ☐ Accept the first intimation of a decision, as the decision!
- ☐ Solve problems for them
- ☐ Talk about your own experience
- ☐ Argue
- ☐ Assume their goals are the same as yours

Self assessment

Facilitator's Worksheet F6.3-4: Action Stage

DESIRED OUTCOME
Change behaviour and increase repertoire of behaviour

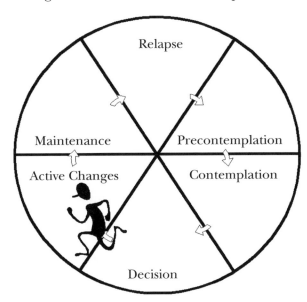

Most useful strategies
- ☐ Remember ambivalence may still be present
- ☐ Monitor small steps
- ☐ Specific feedback
- ☐ Provide a good role model
- ☐ Appropriate information giving.
- ☐ Remove barriers
- ☐ Active helping
- ☐ Celebrate success

Least useful
- ☐ Reflect back when someone wants help or information
- ☐ Assume the problem is solved
- ☐ Over emphasise the negatives of previous behaviour
- ☐ Provide all the solutions
- ☐ Rely only on external rewards

Self assessment

Facilitator's Worksheet F6.3-5: Maintenance

DESIRED OUTCOMES
Maintain the changes
Community reintegration
Relapse prevention

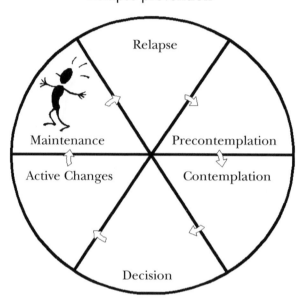

Most useful strategies

- ☐ Be aware when support may still be required, when to let go
- ☐ Build everyday support for the new behaviour
- ☐ Positive feedback on progress
- ☐ Provide an effective role model
- ☐ Affirm and praise
- ☐ Build new skills/ behaviours
- ☐ Plan for coping with lapse
- ☐ Re-enforcement of longer-term goals.

Least useful

- ☐ Let go too early
- ☐ Overemphasis on exploring of previous behaviour
- ☐ Hold them in dependency

Self assessment

Facilitator's Worksheet F6.3-6: If lapse

DESIRED OUTCOME

Learn from experience

Relapse

Maintenance   Precontemplation

Active Changes   Contemplation

Decision

Most useful strategies
- ☐ Frame as part of learning
- ☐ Explore how the lapse occurred and strategies for next time
- ☐ Empathy.
- ☐ Explore ambivalence
- ☐ Explore strengths and who can help.
- ☐ Affirm positives
- ☐ Reflect back self motivating statements concerning desire and confidence to learn from the experience
- ☐ Return to contemplation stage

Least useful
- ☐ Label as their failure
- ☐ See your work as failed
- ☐ Lecture, criticise, blame
- ☐ Give unwanted advice
- ☐ Give up hope

Self assessment and comments

Facilitator's Worksheet F6.3-7:
If maintenance continues

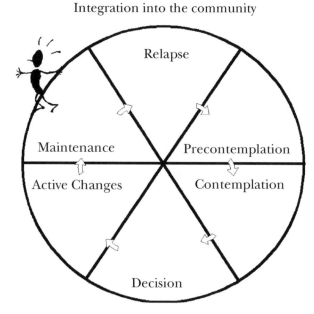

DESIRED OUTCOME
Integration into the community

Most useful strategies
☐ Link to support in the community
☐ Let them go

Facilitator's Worksheet F64: Matching Skills to the Cycle of Change

Draw lines to match the skills to the appropriate stage(s) of change on the cycle.

Skills

- Affirm
- Listen
- Open questions
- Summarise and support 'I want to' statements
- Explore action plans
- Reward changes
- Give advice
- Teach new behaviours
- Provide information
- Remove barriers to change.
- Re-establish optimism

Cycle of Change

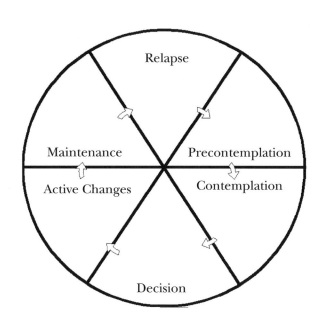

SUMMARY AND APPLICATION

When someone does not really want to change: when they are at pre-contemplation or contemplation stage, advice to change, removing barriers and teaching new behaviours can be counter-productive. At these early stages a motivational approach, that focuses on empathy and developing a sense of unease with present behaviour is particularly helpful. The key skills to do this are to:

Affirm

Listen

Open questions

Summarise

Support self motivating statements

At the later stages additional skills can be used to build on this firm motivational foundation. The chapters that follow explore how you can develop these skills and apply them at the different stages of change.

> 'What people need is a good listening to.'

Motivational work starts with listening and observing. Where the service user is not responding positively, the facilitator needs to ask themselves, 'What is my own level of listening and how can I improve it?'

Listening is particularly important at the early stages of working with someone. It is the foundation of rapport, affirmation and an accurate assessment.

In practice good listening is rare. Consider how the different levels of listening described below apply to your own work. How often are you listened to at the higher levels and what is the impact on you? The power of listening skills alone is probably much underestimated.

FIVE LEVELS OF LISTENING
Level 1 – Limited Listening (preoccupied)

The *desired outcome* of the listener is to 'fix' a problem.

The listener is concentrating on another activity or thought, and occasionally acknowledges the person speaking. Typically, the listener's eyes wander, he fiddles with things, shuffles feet, glances at a watch and so on. David McKee (1980) provides a classic example of this in the story of a young boy Bernard who tells his parents there is a monster in the garden. Every time he starts to explain his parents say 'not now Bernard'. This continues even after the monster eats Bernard. He is told to go to bed and tries in vain to explain he isn't Bernard but a monster.

The listener interrupts, argues, provides advice and continues providing advice despite resistance from the teller ('ah but…'). The listener wants to solve the problem and offers advice or starts taking action before asked. A worker may for instance focus on describing how to cut back on drinking prior to a service user perceiving this as a problem.

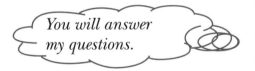

The listener asks question after question after question. If the questions are closed, the teller is likely to provide one-word answers and want to leave within a few minutes. Open questions will at first elicit more information, but even open questions followed only by further questions will start to feel like an interrogation. Less information, more resistance and less willingness to return are likely to be displayed. A worker may fall into this trap when they have an assessment form to complete with a service user, in a limited time.

The listener has made an assessment of the teller prior to the dialogue or within the first few minutes and hears and interprets messages to support this. They listen through the distorted filters of personal prejudices and stereotyping. For example, a worker may assume that a previous report accurately describes the service user.

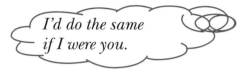

I'd do the same if I were you.

Rather than aiming for empathy and understanding, the listener over-sympathises. 'I would have done the same…' The listener does not explore the whole picture and the possible negative consequences of the behaviour for the teller or others.

The *limitations* of this are poor disclosure and inaccurate information.

Level 2 – Listening to Content

The desired outcome of listener is to hear the facts. The listener:
- is aware of the need to listen
- limits distractions and finds private area to discuss
- makes preparations beforehand to ensure as far as possible the environment is conducive to listening, for example arranging the chairs at a 45° angle rather than directly opposite each other. Ensures there are no barriers between the listener and teller, such as a screen or a table
- hears and notes only the facts of what the teller is saying.

The *limitation* of this is disclosure, but the understanding may be limited.

Level 3 - Active Listening

The *desired outcome* is to build on content listening to facilitate disclosure, and to gain understanding. The listener:

- concentrates on what the teller is saying rather than the next question, or on offering solutions or advice
- unconsciously mirrors some body language, where the teller is willingly and calmly providing information
- displays similar rhythm in the movements to that of the teller (almost like a dance)
- becomes expressive and good-humoured, as does the teller, who then wants to provide information freely.

The *limitations* of this is that over 92% of communication is non-verbal or use of voice; that is, it is body language or the way you say something rather than the actual words you use. To fully understand the other person's perspective, the listener needs to see what isn't said as much as what is.

Level 4 – Empathetic Listening

The *desired outcome* is to build on active listening and gain a clear accurate understanding of:

Situations described

Actions

Mental state – thoughts and feelings

Experiences of all involved.

(Bailey and Egan 1999)

In addition to hearing what is said the listener notices detailed non-verbal reactions and reflects understanding of these to gain accurate empathy (see also below). They notice:

- deletions and generalisations made by the teller
- changes in body movements and posture and rhythms

- changes in facial expression – smiles, frowns, raised eyebrows
- changes in eyes
- changes in automatic responses – breathing, blushing, paleness
- vocal qualities – tone, volume, speed, pauses, silence
- ambiguity of meaning
- indications of feelings.

The listener constantly checks out their own understanding with the teller.

Level 5 – Listening to Develop Discrepancies

The *desired outcome* is to build on the **S.A.M.E.** listening described above, so as to understand core values and beliefs that initially may be unconscious to the teller.

In addition to listening skills the listener reflects the meaning, feeling and discrepancies they have perceived, to check out they have understood correctly. The skills to develop discrepancy are described in Chapter 12.

LISTENING WITH YOUR EYES

Mehrabian (1972) found that communication is made of:

- 8% words
- 34% use of voice
- 58% non-verbal behaviour.

Some cautions on reading body language

Some writers claim to describe universal body language signs that can be interpreted if you are sufficiently skilled. A newspaper quiz showed pictures of eyes and asked readers to rate their own emotional intelligence by guessing what emotion each picture expressed. No context, no supporting signs, no opportunity to know those people and their habitual behaviours. If you photographed the face of an ecstatic fan at a pop concert, and then showed the photo out of context, the expression might be interpreted as terror, rather than extreme excitement.

There *are* trends in human body behaviours that are useful to know as a basis for reading emotions. However, for any one individual there may be a dozen reasons why those signs have been modified to express a different meaning. For example it is not unusual for some people to cry when angry. Different cultures have different body languages.

Body Language and Culture

Balanced eye contact will enhance rapport. However, what is experienced as balanced eye contact between two white able-bodied men may be very different to that between people of different gender or different cultures.

Similarly, how close we stand to people when conversing has important implications. If we stand too far away we may come across as too distant and lacking in interest. What is considered too close and uncomfortable will vary between cultures and genders.

The clothes you choose to wear may be appropriate to the role you have. Clothes will transmit a message. Different faiths and cultures have different ideas about appropriate dress. In particular, when a man and woman are communicating and stepping outside a cultural boundary, this may create unease.

Fine movements such as nodding and shaking of the head communicate messages. You may interpret the former as agreeing and latter as disagreeing. However, Debra Tannen (1992) found that women tend to nod when listening, to encourage the talker to say more, rather than to indicate agreement. In some cultures shaking the head means 'yes' rather than 'no'.

Understand Non-verbal Language by Checking it Out

When something important happens inside, it is often reflected in the body and especially the face, perhaps a small movement of the lips, or a change in the eyes. Humans are programmed to note these small changes in the face. This may not tell us exactly what has happened inside the other person, only that something significant has occurred.

When it seems important, such an observation can be picked up with a reflection 'That seemed painful to you', or 'I noticed you seemed upset', or, better still, describe what you saw. 'You squeezed your eyes shut and your head sank down for a moment.' You can then explore the significance as they experience it, not as you interpret.

Listening to Feelings

You may have been told 'I know how you feel', and experienced it as patronising. No one can really know how someone else feels. A motivational approach would reflect back what was seen, heard and understood. The next chapter (Chapter 8) looks at the art of reflection in detail, but some examples of reflection of non-verbal information are useful here as you think about how you make sense of listening with your eyes.

'I noticed that when you began to talk about John that you started to clench your fist…', or 'Just thinking about the situation seems to bring back feelings of anger'.

As with other reflections, the tone of voice needs to be gentle and reflective rather than accusing. When you reflect your understanding of their feelings, this will often result in the service user saying more. They may elaborate or clarify so that you then have a better picture of their world.

Some workers may feel uncomfortable about discussing feelings, preferring to leave them to others to handle. 'I'm not a counsellor, what if I uncover something I can't handle.' A worker who shies away from feelings may be perceived as unsupportive. Where someone is experiencing strong feelings the need is to listen rather than advise or ignore. When you give someone the space and time to talk through their feelings it helps them to regain control of their lives. This empowers them and helps to increase motivation to change.

Facilitator's Worksheet F7.1: Using Non-verbal Information

How do you respond to each of the pictures below? Use them to practice possible forms of reflections to check out your perception, and to think about the other information you might seek. There are, of course, no right answers; only real people can give you real responses.

The expression	How might you check out your understanding of the expression, by reflecting back?	What other information might you seek
	Example: 'You seem disappointed, as though you hoped for something else.'	Example: Explore how she has been let down. (Might be life, might be this interview.)

F7.1   continued...

	Reflection	Information to Seek

F7.1 continued...

	Reflection	Information to Seek

F7.1   continued...

	Reflection	Information to Seek

F7.1   continued...

	Reflection	Information to Seek

F7.1 continued...

	Reflection	Information to Seek

Photographs used by permission of Phil Taylor and Catherine Fuller, 2007.

The exercises at the end of Chapter 4 on rapport and Chapter 16 on cultivating your motivational skills are also useful to develop listening skills.

SUMMARY

Listening skills cannot be taken for granted. Even when you have excellent listening skills they may be compromised by the circumstances in which you work. Motivational work is built on listening with your eyes and ears: rapport, accurate information, and affirmation depend on it. Good listening is not passive, but needs the listener to engage with the service user. The next chapter shows how the skills of reflection and summarising will enhance listening and build empathy.

Chapter 8

> 'You cannot teach a man anything; you can only help him find it within himself.'
>
> *Galilieo Galilei*

Summarising and reflective listening is the skill of responding to the other person's comment by saying what you understand them to have said. In a skilled facilitator it is an art form that enables the service user to explain their world without the facilitator helping to write their script.

PURPOSES OF REFLECTIVE LISTENING

1. **To clarify**
2. **To let them know what you understand**
3. **To encourage further disclosure**
4. **To encourage ownership**
5. **To highlight discrepancies in desired outcomes**
6. **To shape an interview.**

UNPACKING THE SKILL

Clarify: check out your story of the other person

Humans construct stories to make sense of what they think they know.

Whatever you think you have discerned with your ears and eyes, needs to be checked out by summarising and reflection. Humans are practically incapable of obtaining objective evidence of what is happening in the world, let alone inside another person. In our attempts to make sense of what we see and hear, the information of our five senses is filtered through our brains. Pre-existing ideas and stories cause us to emphasise some evidence and ignore other information. In this way we construct a story to make sense of the evidence. Scientific theories are simply the best story the scientist has that best fits the current evidence. As more evidence comes to light, theories are modified.

You are not dealing in facts, but trying to listen to someone else's reality, and possibly enabling them to see for themselves that their world can be different if they so choose. If your understanding of their world is faulty, they will find it difficult to respond to your work with them. Reflection allows the other person to correct any misunderstanding, thereby enhancing accurate empathy.

Let them Know What you Understand – Empathy

'Empathy is the quality of understanding, as experienced by the service user.'

To express empathy is to allow the other person to know what you understand about them, without judgement. Empathy is not so much a kind of understanding you have of the service user, but rather, *a quality of understanding as experienced by the service user.*

Empathy is both an accurate understanding of what it is like to be the other person, *plus* letting them know what you have understood. It is not enough to know, the other person has to feel understood by you. This can only happen if you have told them what you understand.

Such understanding does not include any judgement on your part, you do not need either to collude or disagree, you simply know something of what it is like for the other person. Reflective listening achieves just that, because you are using only what you have learned from the other person. Nothing of yourself or your own experience is included.

Empathy leaves control, responsibility and decisions entirely with the interviewee. It is the essential building block of motivational skills.

Encourage Further Disclosure

Reflection encourages the service user to say more about themselves.

If you mishear, misunderstand or misinterpret feelings, reflection not only gives opportunity for the other person to correct you, but encourages them to paint a more complete picture of the issue you misunderstood.

How it works

People who are new to reflection often think at first that it sounds patronising, just to repeat back what you have heard. They can feel it takes the interview round in a circle by going over ground already covered. What happens in practice is very different. As the interviewer becomes fluent, the reflection is followed quite naturally by the interviewee saying some more to add to what has been reflected. No question is required after the reflection; just leave it hanging in the air. When done skilfully the conversation flows between the two, but *all* the information comes from the other, the interviewer just reflects (and asks occasional open questions).

Powerful

The approach is so powerful that the other person can sometimes quickly disclose intimate and deeply-held information about themselves. Sometimes they will not be consciously aware of the issues themselves until they say it out loud. Care must be taken that the circumstances and professional purpose of the interview is appropriate to the level of disclosure.

Encourage Ownership

Only they can know what matters to them.

Reflection helps ensure that what is disclosed is not directed by you or your assumptions about the other person's experience. Rather it flows from the storyteller and what is important to them.

You may be constantly surprised by what is said in response to reflection; how the direction of the unfolding story takes an unexpected turn, rarely what you would have guessed or sought to tease out. An intervention, which short-circuits the conversation to the issues that you see as important, will cause the true concerns to remain hidden. When exploring the story and the motivational balance, a reflection, with a few open questions will often lead to the disclosure of what is really important to the other person.

The emphasis on the story being determined only by the other person has another important consequence for motivational work. The storyteller is more able to take responsibility for their own story because all that is said comes from them. Their story is not distorted by our guesses and interruptions. Ownership can be emphasised in the style of reflection, by referring to, 'What you said earlier was…' or 'So what you are saying to me is…'

Highlight Discrepancy

Explore discrepancies using the service user's own words.

As the interview progresses the storyteller owns what is being disclosed and is eventually able to own the disparity between different parts of the story, and especially their stated longer term goals and present behaviours. From this comes a wish and eventual responsibility to change; in other words, motivation to change. The service user can be helped to see their discrepancies, from the facilitator's careful and matter of fact reflection of what they have said. This sort of reflection is always made as information giving, never as an argument for change.

If you attempt to work for solutions, give advice, make judgements or add from your own experience, then responsibility for change flips across to you and the work can be 'ah butted' or argued with by the interviewee. It is difficult for the storyteller to argue if the only material being worked with comes from them and has been checked out with them.

Shape the Interview

> The interview is shaped by what you choose to reflect.

Reflective listening can take a wide variety of forms and styles, mostly to serve different purposes as the interview unfolds. The interview has an aim and a structure. You are concerned to increase motivation by enabling the storyteller to explore the motivational balance. The benefits and loss of staying put and the benefit and loss of changing are explored and eventually the storyteller is helped to contrast these for themselves, and set them against their long-term desires and goals. (See Chapters 11 and 12 for a detailed description of the motivational balance.) Reflection will shape the interview, by what you choose to reflect back, and the style of your reflection. Different kinds of reflections are described below.

Words
Words

Reflect Words
The simplest form is to reflect back the actual words used by the other.

Purpose
Accurate empathy; encourage further disclosure; checking out accuracy.

Meaning
Meaning

Reflect Meaning
To reflect back in your own words, the meaning you have gathered so far.

Purpose
Accurate empathy; encourage further disclosure about the meaning; checking out accuracy of understood meaning; focus interview on some aspect of the meaning.

Non-Verbal
Non-Verbal

Reflect Non-verbal Information

To reflect back what you have noticed that may be significant.

Purpose

To understand non-verbal signals that seem significant to you.

To check out any interpretation you have made of non-verbal information.

To show that you are sensitive to the whole person and the way they express their concerns in other ways than words.

Emotions
Emotions

Reflect Emotions

To reflect back emotion and feelings.

Purpose

We cannot mind-read but we often guess or feel sensitive to others' (presumed) emotions. You may need to check out your interpretation of their feelings; to encourage more disclosure of feelings; to focus on one particular feeling or emotion.

Focus
Focus

Focus

To focus on one aspect (words or tone of voice).

Purpose

Can result in the other person drawing back from an

exaggerated meaning to a position they really own; can be used to emphasise one aspect or to focus the interview.

Summarising the Story so Far

To summarise what has been said so far in the interview or since the last summary, or at the last meeting.

Purpose

A way to start a subsequent interview or round off a current interview.

Useful to recap at any time, especially if the interviewer is not sure where to go next. Will often be followed by more disclosure. If this explores a new area, the interviewee has chosen where to go next. If repetition then this may indicate the area of ambivalence. Regular summaries help the interviewee to feel understood (empathy) as well as keep track of the direction and story so far.

Selective summary

Purpose

Used to draw attention to some aspects, and guide the interview.

Summarise
Summarise

Summarise
Summarise

Summarise
Summarise

A balancing summary
Sets out pros and cons understood so far.

Purpose
A summary of goals that seeks to draw out the discrepancy between present behaviour and long-term goals. Can produce a self-motivating statement. The summary should emphasise their words, 'earlier you said…', 'but you also …

The Art of
The Art of
Reflection
Reflection

The Art of Reflection
Using all these types in part or in mixture, together with your own style becomes an art form. This is the skill used in following through the exploration of the issues, the ambivalence, the motivational balance, short- and long-term goals and to help the other see the discrepancies for themselves.

Even simple practice of the above will produce worthwhile results.

Facilitator's Worksheet F8.1: Group Training Exercise in Summarising and Reflective Listening

This simple exercise is especially useful for facilitators who are new to the art of reflection. The exercise helps people grasp what a reflection is and demonstrates how reflections are experienced as helpful by those on the receiving end. A minimum of five people and an exercise leader are needed.

The Exercise

1. Invite a volunteer from the group to describe, for two or three minutes, something they are either ambivalent about or a piece of work they are stuck with. An alternative might be to describe their journey to work that morning. You are only looking for a brief description. Before they tell their story explain that you are going to ask some people to listen very carefully to what has been said and to reflect back in different ways. It is important the listeners are positioned so that they can see the storyteller, or they will not be able to listen with eyes and ears.

2. After the story each reflector is asked to turn to the storyteller and give their reflection directly to them. The storyteller can respond in any way they wish. (The exercise leader should note down any responses.)

*   The first person offers the speaker a simple reflection of the *content*
*   The next person summarises the *meaning*
*   The next reflects back any piece of *non-verbal* behaviour they have noticed
*   The next reflects back the *feelings* they think they have understood
*   The fifth *focuses* on just on one aspect of what was said.

3. When all five have reflected back, ask the storyteller about their response to the feedback they have received. Check if they felt understood (accurate empathy). Check if the issue was clarified for them in any way. Give positive feedback to good examples of reflection. Add any of your own observations on the way the listener responded to reflection.

4. Repeat the exercise asking the person next in line to describe something as above, and asking the next four people to reflect as previously. Take feedback and repeat the exercise until all have had an opportunity to reflect including those who told their stories.

5. Draw out what was helpful. The exercise leader should take note of any interesting responses to illustrate how reflection helps someone to express their own world experience. For instance, the storyteller may correct the reflector, may give more information, or may just nod when the emotion is correctly described.

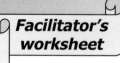

Facilitator's Worksheet F8.2:
A Reflective Listening Exercise Part 1
Possible meanings

The essence of reflective listening is to reflect your perceived understanding. For the following statements suggest some possible different meanings that you might reflect.

1. That's doing my head in.

1. (*meanings*)

2. I'm not a racist.

2. (*meanings*)

3. Perphaps it was not a good idea.

3. (*meanings*)

Facilitator's Worksheet F8.3:
Reflective Listening Exercise Part 2
Possible reflections

Having considered possible meanings above, now jot down how you might word an actual reflection as a response to the following statements.

1. That's doing my head in.

1.

2. I'm not a racist.

2.

3. Perphaps it was not a good idea.

3.

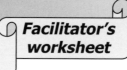

Facilitator's Worksheet F8.4: Some Possible Meanings for F8.2

Note, there are no right answers; only those that might prove accurate for one unique person.

1. That's doing my head in.

I don't understand any of this.

I am confused.

I'm getting angry.

I feel upset and hurt.

I've started to realise there is an alternative way of looking at this.

I've always thought what I was doing was ok and now I don't know.

I need some space to think about this.

2. I'm not a racist.

I don't want to be labelled.

I don't think I'm prejudiced against black people.

I don't want you to think I'm racist.

I wouldn't want to be a bigot.

I don't really agree with racism although some of what I do is racist.

F84   continued...

> 3. Perphaps it was not a good idea.

I'm feeling uncomfortable with my behaviour.

Possibly other people were hurt by it.

There may have been some disadvantages.

I could have done something different.

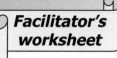

Facilitator's Worksheet F8.5:
Some Possible Reflections for F8.2

Note, there are no right answers; only those which are more useful.

1. That's doing my head in.

1. (Reflection)

You need some space to think about it.

2. I'm not a racist.

2. (Reflection)

You feel labels are not very helpful.

3. Perphaps it was not a good idea.

3. (Reflection)

It sounds like you think there were other things you could have done which would have been more helpful.

SUMMARY

The important thing is to notice what response you get and to change tack when it is unhelpful, especially if there are 'ah buts' and arguments – it takes two to argue! Reflective listening is really the heart of motivational skills. It is the non-confrontational way of achieving confrontation between short- and long-term goals. Reflective listening can be supplemented by the careful use of open questions and these are discussed in the next chapter.

> 'The beginning of knowledge is the discovery of something
> we do not understand.'
>
> *Frank Herber*

The integration of open questions into a dialogue can be a useful way of drawing out more information and increasing the desire to change. To be effective, questions need to be asked alongside the other skills of listening and reflecting. Questions are most effective when the facilitator genuinely values the individual and desires to understand.

WHAT ARE OPEN QUESTIONS?

The above is an open question. It cannot easily be answered with a one-word answer. It requires the person reading or hearing the question to think and to provide a longer answer.

> Do you know what open questions are?

Even though the question is answered 'Yes', further open questions are needed to discover exactly what is understood by an 'open question'. Closed questions are questions that can be answered by 'yes' or 'no', for example, 'Do you...?', 'Have you thought about...?', 'Will you...?'

Examples of Closed Questions

A closed question would be:

Although this appears to be a clear commitment we have no idea what the service user has actually understood or how the 'yes' might be qualified by reservations, ambivalence and misunderstanding.

When students are asked what open questions are, often the first boardstorm of answers are:

- Where?
- Who?
- When?

- Why?
- What?
- How?

However, when discussed further it is clear that 'Who?', 'Where?', 'When?' and 'How much?' are only semi-open questions, because they more often than not elicit one or two word answers. These kinds of questions can still be used for checking out knowledge of specific facts and to provide greater evidence of understanding and reinforcement of information.

Examples of Semi-open Questions

Fully open questions are used to elicit more detailed information about individuals' thinking and feelings. In this way we can begin to explore someone else's world. These questions often begin with:

What?
Tell me about?
How did this happen?
How do you feel?

Without the inclusion of open questions and reflective listening, the barriers to and merits of attending the programme may not have been recognised or voiced by the recipient. The voicing of reasons to change is a fundamental purpose of open questions.

Why 'Why' Questions Do Not Always Work

An important part of assessment and helping people to change is to find out the reasons and motivators for their current behaviour. The first question we usually think of is 'Why?'

'Why?' questions are open questions, but can have unintended overtones of criticism. Many will remember being asked as a child, when something has gone wrong, 'Why did you do that?' You are asked to explain something which by implication is your fault.

'Why?' questions can be difficult to answer. Children, parents and clients frequently reply, 'I don't know, it just happened'. The questions assume you had a clear reason.

If this is the reply, try reframing the question to a 'What is it about that…?', 'Tell me about…', or a 'How…?' question.

So if you ask, 'Why did you smoke with your friends?' and are told, 'I don't know, it just happened' or 'Everybody does it', try:

What was it about your friends that you chose to smoke?

What were you thinking when the others smoked?

Tell me exactly what happened just before you took a cigarette?

Reflection and open questions may then be used to explore the whole story in depth to understand the other person's world. With this more accurate understanding you can then use targeted open questions and begin to explore alternative thinking and behaviours.

We have seen that the two functions of open questions are firstly, to draw out more information, and secondly, to check understanding of expectations. A clear, accurate assessment of an individual's situation, thinking and feelings is the first step in identifying factors linked with the problem area.

A further valuable use of open questions is to elicit both the desire to change and the confidence to change. Open questions can be used in what is called a 'socratic way' within the cycle of change framework to achieve this. These kinds of open questions are discussed in Chapter 12.

Requests for Information (TED)

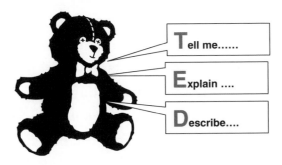

Tell me......

Explain ....

Describe....

Asking for information can work in exactly the same way as an open question. A request is often included as an example of an open question, albeit that grammatically it is an imperative. The voice tone and context will determine whether it is experienced as an 'open question' or a demand for information.

The words 'Please will you?' are left out, because if you include them, the sentence becomes a closed question! What matters most, as in all conversations, is not the exact form of words, but the manner in which they are spoken and the response you get.

Weaving Open Questions and Reflections Seamlessly Together

Open questions, however well asked, are a form of interrogation. If question after question is asked the service user will quickly feel under interrogation, rather than being invited to share their concerns. As a rough guide ask no more than three questions in a row. Voice tone and non-verbal messages are equally important in avoiding a sense of interrogation. Skilled facilitators can draw out information, concerns and motivation by using just reflections. Below is an example of weaving questions and reflections together.

Examples of open questions used with reflections

Facilitator: **Great, it sounds like you are clear about how often and who you need to see. [*Reflection*] What's your understanding of what happens when you go? [*Open question*]**

Service user: Well the person who sent me said something about going on one of these thinking courses.

Facilitator: **Yes, that's right, the enhanced thinking programme will be offered as well as some individual work with me. You seem a little unsure about it. [*Reflection, information, reflection*]**

Service user: Jason, my social worker says they meet as a group each week and do lots of exercises, talk about problems and other things they could have done, but I don't understand what I might get out of it.

Facilitator: **So, you are aware that it involves meeting as a group exploring thinking skills and problem solving. It sounds like your social worker thought it would be right for you, but you are wondering what changes it might highlight for you. [*Reflection*]**

Service user: Yes, I don't really understand what thinking I need to change.

Facilitator: **What would you like to be different about your life? [*Open question*]**

Service user: Well I'd prefer not to have to come here.

Facilitator: **And what would stop you from needing to come here again? [*Open question*]**

Service user: Getting my life in order, I suppose, but it just seems to mess up on its own.

Facilitator: **So things just seem to happen to you rather than you being in control. [*Reflection*]**

Service user: Well yes, or I just make the wrong decisions over and over again.

Facilitator: **So you would like to be able to think more clearly and stop making decisions which eventually lead to things going wrong for you. [*Summarising*]**

Service user: Yes that's right … so if I change my thinking I can get more control over my life. [*Self-motivational statement*]

Facilitator: **You mentioned you were not sure you would always attend. What might stop you from attending? [*Reflection plus open question*]**

Service user: I don't think I can afford to get there and what happens if I get a job?

Facilitator: **(Asks about barriers to attending and explores together how these can be overcome.)**
So in summary let's write down what the costs and benefits you see in attending and consequences for you if you don't complete the programme.

Service user: (Outlines in more details benefits of attending and costs to self and others of not completing.)

Facilitator: **How are you feeling now? [*Open question*]**

Service user: A lot less scared than I was, but a little anxious.

Facilitator: **What do you think would help? [*Open question*]**

Service user: I think I will talk to Jason a bit more and I will get him to show me where the programme building is so I can find it.

Facilitator: **Good, it sounds like you have a clearer understanding of what the programme will offer you and what you can offer to it. What other questions have you at the moment? [*Reflection and open question. NB A closed question would have been 'Have you any questions?' – prompting a 'No'*]**

Service user: Yes, thanks. I do feel clearer about the programme. Oh, just one other question. I've heard that I've got to have a psycho test. What's that all about?

Interview continues…

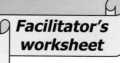

Facilitator's Worksheet F9.1: Open Questions

Reframe the following closed questions and statements as open questions.

1. Is accommodation likely to be a problem to you?

Open question 1.

2. Do you need help with basic skills?

Open question 2.

3. Have you got any money problems?

Open question 3.

4. Have you had any difficulties with relationships?

Open question 4.

5. Do you have any difficulties associated with drink or drugs?

Open question 5.

F9.1 continued...

6. Have you got any mental health difficulties?	*Open question 6.*

7. Do you have any difficulties with solving problems?	*Open question 7.*

8. Do you have any difficulties with self-control?	*Open question 8.*

9. Do you enjoy your work?	*Open question 9.*

10. Have you any particular needs that are not being met?	*Open question 10.*

F9.1 continued...

11. Are you OK?

Open question 11.

12. Will you attend the programme?

Open question 12.

13. You know what will happen to you if you don't take your medicine regularly, don't you?

Open question 13.

14. You've missed an appointment. If you miss another appointment I will take you back to court.

Open question 14.

15. Have you any questions?

Open question 14.

Facilitator's Worksheet F9.2: Possible Open Questions Solutions to Facilitator's Worksheet F9.1

There are no right answers. These are some examples.

1. Is accommodation likely to be a problem to you?

> Open question 1.
> *Tell me about your accommodation and any problems you may have re will sleep this week?*

2. Do you need help with basic skills?

> Open question 2.
> *How do you get on when you have to fill in forms or have stuff to read?*

3. Have you got any money problems?

> Open question 3.
> *What money problems do you have, if any?*

4. Have you had any difficulties with relationships?

> Open question 4.
> *Tell me about the people who matter most to you.*

5. Do you have any difficulties associated with drink or drugs?

> Open question 5.
> *Tell me about any problems you have had linked with drink or drugs.*

F9.2 continued...

6. Have you got any mental health difficulties?

Open question 6.
How would you describe your mental health?
What medication are you taking?

7. Do you have any difficulties with solving problems?

Open question 7.
How well do you solve problems?
Which problems do you find difficult to cope with?

8. Do you have any difficulties with self-control?

Open question 8.
Tell me about times when you have felt you have lost control.
What other situations do you find difficult?

9. Do you enjoy your work?

Open question 9.
How do you feel about your work?

10. Have you any particular needs that are not being met?

Open question 10.
What needs have you got that are not being met?

F9.2 continued...

11. Are you OK?	*Open question 11.* *How are you?*
12. Will you attend the programme?	*Open question 12.* *What might stop you from attending?* *How can you address these?* *What are the benefits of attending?*
13. You know what will happen to you if you don't take your medicine regularly, don't you?	*Open question 13.* *What do you think will happen if you don't take your medicine regularly?*
14. You've missed an appointment. If you miss another appointment I will take you back to court.	*Open question 14.* *What do you think will happen if you miss an appointment again?*
15. Have you any questions?	*Open question 15.* *What else would you like to know?*

SUMMARY

When used selectively and with reflections, open questions are a useful tool to help unpack the service user's concerns. More complex open questions are discussed in Chapter 11. The next chapter will show ways to use skilful listening, reflections and open questions to work with resistance and avoid argument.

Chapter 10

'Was it something I said? Or something I did?'

Chapters 7 and 8 discussed how communication between two people can go wrong. Either person can misinterpret the behaviour of the other and assume something that was not intended.

In Chapter 10 we will explore how, as a skilled facilitator you can learn to observe accurately the response you get and then if necessary change your behaviour to get a different response. In this way you create rapport and engage service users in work that may be initially challenging and uncomfortable for them, prior to achieving the changes they want.

You can change your behaviour to get a different response.

The motivational skills explored in this toolkit are based on the experience and research of 'what works' in gaining helpful responses from people who are initially resistant to change. The crucial underlying skill is to be aware of the effects you create in others. Learn what works, or try out new approaches. In this way you continuously add to your repertoire throughout your life.

**There is no failure,
only feedback.**

*All experience is
information.*

MOTIVATIONAL SKILLS ARE EVIDENCE-BASED PRACTICE IN ACTION

The evidence of the results of your practice is happening here and now in front of you. All this comes for free; you only have to observe the responses you get.

For example, if the person resists, this is evidence that you need to change your tack – probably more listening and reflection. If they give you more information that is evidence that your intervention is effective at drawing out information. If they make a self-motivating statement, it is evidence that you have helped to develop discrepancy. The trick is always to be aware of how the other person is responding to what you are doing.

Behaviour is …
the highest quality information.

Roadblocks

Thomas Gordon (1970) refers to interventions from the facilitator, which hinder change, as 'roadblocks'. Often the facilitator uses these for the best of intentions in an attempt to 'fix' a problem immediately. The facilitator sees a problem and immediately offers advice, solutions, probes or lectures.

Instead of empowering the service user to change, these interventions block change. The facilitator disempowers the service user by assuming a one-up position, stopping dialogue or facilitating argument. Unfortunately, the facilitator may continue to provide the roadblocks despite the resistance, in the belief that eventually they will fix the problem.

> 'There is nothing which we receive with so much reluctance as advice.'
>
> *Joseph Addison*

Some road blocks after Thomas Gordon

NO ROUTE AHEAD - ROAD BLOCKED

Warning/threatening

Moralising/preaching

Judging/criticising/blaming

Shaming/ridicule

Ordering/directing/commanding

Arguing/lecturing/advice

Example of some road blocks in action:

Service user: I drove the car whilst disqualified just after my partner had been having a right go at me. I wouldn't have driven the car if it wasn't for her.

Facilitator: **You need to take responsibility for your own actions.**

Service user: Ah but, you don't know what she's like, it's her who should be here.

Giving feedback on behaviour may sometimes work by creating doubt, but it may also be met with resistance, especially at the contemplation stage.

Service user: I'm not an alcoholic.

Facilitator: **Possibly not, but you are drinking quite a lot.** [*criticising*]

Service user: Ah but, not that much.

Facilitator: **Well, a lot more than is helpful to your health or your behaviour. It is recommended that you only drink 14 units a week. You are drinking a lot more than that and getting into a lot of trouble as a result.** [*arguing, advice, lecturing*]

Service user: How do you know? This was just a one off.

The starting point for handling resistant behaviour is to become aware of the effect of your own behaviour.

Whatever you resist…

       …*persists*

Do something different…

       …*anything*

If you find yourself caught up in an argument or someone becomes defensive, you need to change your behaviour to get a different response. You can switch to different skills and tactics.

Some Resistant Behaviours and How to Respond

ARGUING

- Service user contests the accuracy, expertise or integrity of the worker

- Response:
  - Socratic question of evidence
  - reflective listening

It is surprisingly easy to slip into an argument. If you disagree or feel you need to correct something that has been said, you can state a different point of view. Suddenly you are debating and then arguing. This increases resistance.

Using Socratic Questions

Instead of making statements, or giving advice to contradict resistance, Socrates, the fifth century BC philosopher, asked questions that led the speaker to present the arguments for change themselves. These have since been called 'Socratic questions'. Miller and Rollnick (2002) have used such questions along with reflections to turn the energy of resistance back on itself to intiate change: 'to roll with resistance'. Helpful Socractic questions focus on :

- What's the alternative…?
- What if …?
- What's the evidence?
- What consequences?

To be effective a Socratic question is used in conjunction with careful listening and reflections. Where the response to Socratic questioning is more resistance, it is often helpful to increase the use of reflections and decrease the number of questions. The aim is for the service user to work at the issue themselves without you imposing your view.

If the argument is about your integrity or the basis of your work together try exploring what was expected from the contract.

INTERRUPTIONS

- **Service user breaks in and interrupts in a defensive manner**
- **Response:**
  - **reflective listening**
  - **change focus**
  - **reflect any discrepancy**

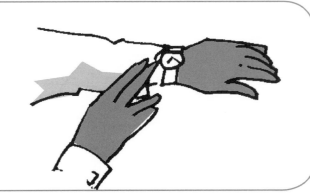

You may have your own train of thought and questions as you explore the other person's world. If the service user interrupts, you can see this as either disruptive, or you can see it as the service user wishing to offer you more information about their world.

If this is clearly a diversion from the purpose try changing focus by Socratic open questions or a selective summary of what has been said so far. Sometimes the interruption when listened to gives information about discrepancy between the present concerns and the longer term aspirations.

DENYING

- **Not wishing to recognise a problem, co-operate, accept responsibility, or take advice**
- **Response:**
  - **stop giving advice!**
  - **reflective listening**
  - **emphasise personal choice and control**

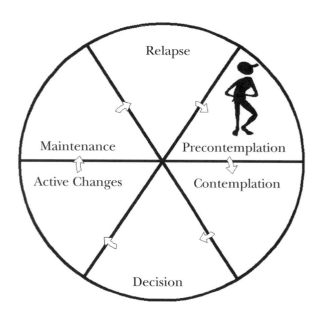

What appears to be 'denial' is often a normal stage in the change process which occurs prior to feeling ready to contemplate change (precontemplation), rather than a personality trait. The facilitator can exacerbate the position by giving advice or using some of the classic roadblocks described above. On the other hand, appropriate Socratic questions and reflective listening can help the facilitator to understand the service user's reasons for wanting to stay the same. This will emphasise the service user's personal control, highlight inconsistencies and makes it safer for them to move into contemplation.

IGNORING

Inattention: not following or attending to the worker.

- **Side-tracking**
- **Changing the direction of the conversation**
- **Response:**
  - **reflective listening**
  - **reflect on the silence and the observed feelings**

Some people are skilled at ignoring or sidetracking and use this as a tactic. Others may find it hard to concentration and have a small attention span. Adapt your communication to suit the service user.

A reflective response to sidetracking may seem to collude with it, but it can create empathy, emphasise personal control and give opportunity for summary or Socratic questions to redirect the focus.

Manage resistance…

…by changing tack

- Use Socratic questions
- Reflect or summerise
- Find a new focus
- Emphasise personal choices and control
- Highlight discrepencies

The key to handling resistance is to be always aware of the response of the other person and how this relates to your own behaviour. Practise changing tack by employing some of the skills listed above. You may also need to pay attention to your non-verbal behaviour and your voice tones. Remember resistance may be an attempt to get you to listen to information about the other person's world that you have not yet explored.

> See **Chapter 12** for more on drawing out discrepencies

Take a break. Sometimes you are tired and you may need to break the cycle of resistance by ending the interview. This gives opportunity to summarise what has happened so far, by way of closing the piece of work. You can then think through, or discuss with others, tactics for the next meeting. It is sometimes useful to come right into the here and now and reflect on what is happening between you; What feelings and behaviours are you observing?

Example of a Motivational Approach

Service user: I drove whilst disqualified just after my partner had been having a real go at me. I wouldn't have done it if it wasn't for her.

Facilitator: **So in some ways you blame your partner for what has happened. [*reflection*]**

Service user: Well to a certain extent, although not totally I suppose.

Facilitator: **Not totally. [*selective reflection of discrepancy with blaming partner*]**

Service user: Well I got disqualified in the first place.

Facilitator: **Tell me about that. [*open question*]**

Service user: Excess alcohol.

Facilitator: **You'd been drinking and driving on a number of occasions. [*reflecting meaning*]**

Service user: Yeah – it's not a problem though. I'm not an alcoholic.

Facilitator: **You don't want to have unhelpful labels attached to you and you're not even sure if alcohol has caused you any problems. [*reflecting meaning*]**

Service user: Well, if I hadn't drunk the booze I would still have my licence and wouldn't be here. [*self motivating statement – problem clarification*]

Facilitator: **So, one consequence of drinking has been that you can't drive any more and you have a criminal record. What other consequencs have there been for you? [*Reflection of discrepancy and Socratic question about consequences*]**

Service user: I've been drinking alcohol ever since I can remember. My dad drank, my mates all drink and I do as well. I don't really think there's anything wrong with it and never have, it's just that my partner says she's fed up with the court cases and that sort of thing and I thought perhaps I should drink a bit less.

Facilitator: **So drinking alcohol is something that has been part of your lifestyle for some time. On the one hand you think it's OK, but on the other you are concerned about the effect that it is having upon your partner and upon your own behaviour.** [*reflection of discrepancy*]

Service user: Yeah…It would be difficult to change, but I do love Ruth and she's been threatening to go for sometime. I'm also frightened that if I get another court conviction that I will lose my job. I might go to prison and then where would I be. I'm really quite concerned about my drinking [*self-motivating statement – identifying concerns*].

Style and Response

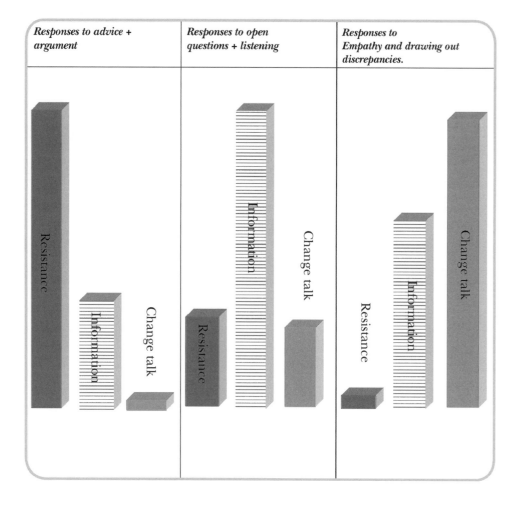

The above diagram shows typical responses you can expect when using different approaches with people who feel ambivalent about, or do not want to change, a behaviour.

- *Arguing or advice:* Response = lots of resistance, some information, little change talk
- *Open questions and listening:* Response = some resistance, lots of information, some change talk
- *Empahty and drawing out discrepancies:* Response = less resistance, good information, much more change talk

Facilitator's Worksheet F10.1

Suggest how you might encourage a service user to question their own 'resistant' statements below by using:

a) a reflection

b) a Socratic open question.

1. 'I forgot'

> *Reflection:*
>
> *Open Question:*

2. 'You're a really good social worker, but those programme tutors are useless.'

> *Reflection:*
>
> *Open Question:*

3. 'She didn't put up much of a fight so she obviously wanted to have sex with me.'

> *Reflection:*
>
> *Open Question:*

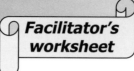

F10.1 continued...

4. 'She purposely left the top of the ketchup bottle half off so that it would spray over me and I would look stupid. I only made it clear that I wasn't to be fooled with.'

> *Reflection:*
>
> *Open Question:*

5. 'Everyone hates all of those people anyway. They are all likely to attack us at any moment if we don't do it first.'

> *Reflection:*
>
> *Open Question:*

6. 'It just happened'

> *Reflection:*
>
> *Open Question:*

Facilitator's Worksheet F10.2

Possible reflections to encourage consideration of change for the statements in worksheet F10.1 above. There are no right answers; some useful suggestions are made below.

1. 'I forgot.'

> *Reflection:*
>
> **You did not remember to take your medicine on this occasion.**
> *The reflection implies that forgetting was a specific happening on a specific occasion and opens the way to further exploration of what could be done differently.*

2. 'You're a really good social worker, but those programme tutors are useless.'

> *Reflection:*
>
> **So you are wondering how the programme will be of use to you.**
> *Reflection of the meaning you perceive. The purpose is to draw out how useful the programme could be.*

3. 'She didn't put up much of a fight so she obviously wanted to have sex with me.'

> *Reflection:*
>
> **You wouldn't want to have sex with someone who was unwilling and you would have known she was unwilling if you had had to use more force.**
> *Reflection of meaning. The purpose is for the interviewee to hear the discrepancy between values and behaviour.*

F10.2 continued...

4. 'She purposely left the top of the ketchup bottle half off so that it would spray over me and I would look stupid. I only made it clear that I wasn't to be fooled with.'

> *Reflection:*
>
> **As you see it, you were hurt a lot more than she was.**
> Slightly exaggerated reflection delivered as a statement not a question. The purpose is to raise doubt.

5. 'Everyone hates all of those people anyway. They are all likely to attack us at any moment if we don't do it first.'

> *Reflection:*
>
> **So you know of no one who would have behaved differently.**
> *Reflection of meaning – purpose to raise doubt.*
>
> or
>
> **So you are feeling angry and perhaps a little scared.**
> *Reflection of feeling – purpose to gain a more information before developing discrepancy.*

6. 'It just happened.'

> *Reflection:*
>
> **You cannot think of anything you did beforehand.**
> *Reflection of meaning, delivered as a gentle statement not as a question. Purpose to develop discrepancy.*

Facilitator's Worksheet F10.3

Possible Socratic open questions to roll with resistance for the statements in F10.1 above. There are no right answers; some useful suggestions are made below.

1. 'I forgot.'

> *Open questions:*
>
> **Tell me what you were doing beforehand?**
> **What were you thinking?**
> **How could you have done this differently?**

2. 'You're a really good social worker, but the programme is useless.'

> *Open questions:*
>
> **What do you mean by useless?**
> **Tell me what has caused you to feel this way?**
> **Your mate, John has finished the programme. What would he say?**

3. 'She didn't put up much resistance so she obviously wanted to have sex with me.'

> *Open questions:*
>
> **What do you mean by 'didn't put up much resistance?'**
> **What else might she have been thinking?**

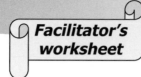

F10.3 continued...

4. 'She purposely left the top of the ketchup bottle half off so that it would spray over me and I would look stupid. I only made it clear that I wasn't to be fooled with.'

> *Open questions:*
>
> **How did you make it clear?**
> **What could be another explanation for the top being loose?**

5. 'Everyone hates all of those people anyway.'

> *Open* questions:
>
> **Who do you mean by everyone?**
> **What evidence have you got that that is the case?**

6. 'It just happened.'

> *Open questions:*
>
> **Tell me exactly how it happened on this occasion**
> **What could you have prevented it this time?**

Facilitator's worksheet

Facilitator's Worksheet F10.4: Responses to resistance

Suggest some alternative facilitator responses that might avoid argument.

---

1. Arguing
Service user: 'Well cannabis doesn't have any bad effects for my mates and me.

Facilitator's reply

---

2. Denial
Service user: 'I manage quite well thanks, I know how to cope with my illness, it's just that others get upset.'

Facilitator's reply

---

3. Ignoring
Facilitator: 'Tell me more about your concern over Lucy.'
Service user: 'I am sorry I was late, the buses in this town are awful.'

Facilitator's reply

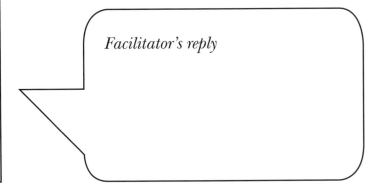

F10.4 continued...

4. Interrupting

Facilitator: (third attempt) 'It's important we discuss what work we can do together, my role is…'
Service user (breaking in again): 'Did you see the Stones concert on telly last night? Best…'

Facilitator's reply

5. 'Ah but' and advice

Facilitator: 'We find what works best is to practice regularly every morning.'
Service user. 'I only have time to dress and get the train.'
Facilitator: 'It would be worth getting up half an hour early, it's important to practice first thing.'
Service user: 'Its more important for me to get my sleep and get to work on time.'

Facilitator's reply

6. Judging

Facilitator: 'That was not a good idea.'
Service user: 'It was a bloody good idea.'

Facilitator's reply

Facilitator's Worksheet F10.5: Some Possible Replies to F10.4

There are no right answers: each reply will produce a different response.

1. Arguing

Service user: 'Well cannabis doesn't have any bad effects for my mates and me.

Facilitator's reply:
So you don't know any body who has difficulties linked to cannabis.

What's the worst thing you have heard cannabis can do to people?

2. Denial

Service user: 'I manage quite well thanks, I know how to cope with my illness, it's just that others get upset.'

Facilitator's reply:
Tell me how it upsets others.

3. Ignoring

Facilitator: 'Tell me more about your concern over Lucy.'
Service user: 'I am sorry I was late, the buses in this town are awful.'

Facilitator's reply:
Thank you for apologising, sounds like your concerns about getting here make it difficult to focus on your concerns about Lucy.

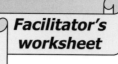

F10.5 continued...

4. Interrupting

Facilitator: (third attempt) 'It might be helpful if we clarify what are roles are.'

Service user (breaking in again): 'Did you see the stones concert on telly last night? Best...'

Facilitator's reply:
I am wondering if you are ready to talk about our work together.

5. 'Ah but' and advice

Facilitator: 'We find what works best is to practice regularly every morning'

Service user: 'I only have time to dress and get the train.'

Facilitator: 'It might be worth getting up half an hour early, it is important to practice first thing.'

Service user: 'Its more important for me to get my sleep and get to work on time.'

Facilitator's reply:
Managing to get sleep and to work on time is also really important to you, and you do not want to upset the routine which works for you.

5. Judging

Facilitator: 'That was not a good idea.'

Service user: 'It was a bloody good idea.'

Facilitator's reply:
Tell me more about the idea and what you hoped from it.

Facilitator's Worksheet F10.6: Your agency

How do you think service users rate your agency on the continuum below?

Confrontational ┼┼┼┼┼┼┼┼┼┼┼┼┼┼┼┼┼┼┼┼┼┼┼┼┼┼┼┼┼┼┼┼┼┼┼┼Motivational

Some roadblocks

- **Warning/threating** |
- **Moralising/preaching**
- **Judging/ criticising /blaming**
- **Shaming/ ridicule**
- **Ordering/directing/commanding**
- **Arguing/ lecturing**

(Thomas Gordon 1970)

All changes involves a loss

Affirm

Listen

Open questions

Summaries

Self motivating statements

Where on the continuum below do you think your own style lies?

Confrontational┼┼┼┼┼┼┼┼┼┼┼┼┼┼┼┼┼┼┼┼┼┼┼┼┼┼┼┼┼┼┼┼┼┼┼┼Motivational

SUMMARY

Resistance and argument can arise at any stage and indicate that either the facilitator needs to listen more or the service user is still ambivalent about the matter in hand. It is the facilitator's responsibility to use their skills to avoid argument. The next chapter will look at the nature of ambivalence and some of the ways in which it can be resolved.

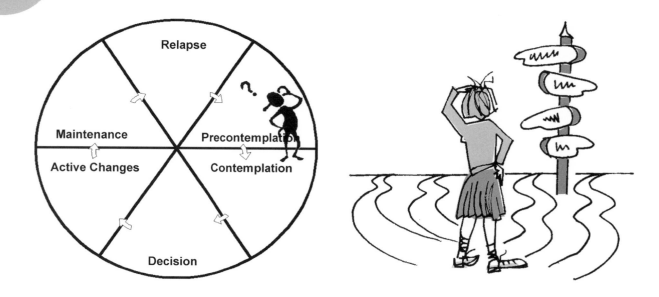

'I am in two minds about what to do.'

Dilemmas are part of life and mostly people can find a way through. However, some kinds of dilemmas are characterised by strong ambivalence, literally the presence of two opposing emotions. The word ambivalence is often used to describe a state of inaction or indecision. This is in fact the result of the ambivalence and may be experienced by others as a lack of motivation.

This chapter explores the nature of ambivalence and how that informs the way you help someone build a motivational balance. Understanding and working with ambivalence is central to motivational work, from initiating consideration of change, to clarifying reasons for change, to decision making and action.

AMBIVALENCE

- **Is OK and natural**
- **Ambivalence causes us to explore**
- **Facilitators work with ambivalence**

THE NATURE OF AMBIVALENCE

All of us are ambivalent about some things some of the time. It's OK to be ambivalent. Often it's useful to be ambivalent because this causes us to explore the pros and cons of a situation before deciding on action. There are at least three kinds of ambivalence.

1. The joy-joy dilemma

In this situation you have to choose between two good things such as two job offers of similar salary and position. Most of us would be able to weigh up the finer pros and cons and make a decision.

2. The pain-pain dilemma

Otherwise known as being between a rock and a hard place, in this kind of dilemma, whatever you do will cause you anxiety or strife. The trick here is to weigh up the least damaging option or find a third way.

3. The joy-pain dilemma

In this situation if you choose one path you will lose something valuable, but gain something you need. On the other hand, if you choose the other path you will keep the thing you value, but lose something you need. This is a double whammy. Whatever you do, you both gain and lose.

Trying to work out the pros and cons, with gains and losses on one side and gains and losses on the other side is very confusing. You are likely to find that you move back and forth over the issues in your head in a never-ending circle, unable to make a decision and so become stuck with the behaviour that is the current habit. This is the kind of dilemma that leads to stuck behaviour and which is best addressed by motivational skills. It is the kind of dilemma experienced by addicts, and many who habitually continue with harmful behaviours.

The motivational balance is a simple tool that can be used to help somebody weigh up the pros and cons of such a dilemma. The diagram below is a simplified version of a motivational balance, where you can write down the factors on each side of the balance, as part of a motivational interview. The list is especially useful for people with visual learning styles. You can also have it as a concept in your mind in order to encourage the interviewee to talk about both sides of the balance.

MOTIVATIONAL 	BALANCE
Reasons I want to stay as I am	**Reasons I want to change**

Four Voices

The most disabling ambivalence has, as it were, four competing voices in the head: a pros voice and a cons voice for each possible action. The four voices are all shouting at once, and if any voice is winning, the others will argue all the harder. Often it is easier to choose to stay the same by simply doing nothing. Sometimes the current habits also blocks out the anxiety caused by the dilemma.

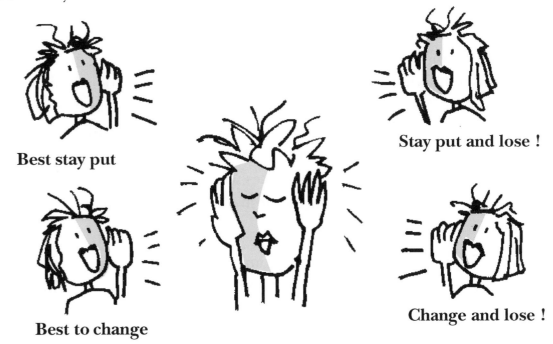

Best stay put

Stay put and lose !

Best to change

Change and lose !

However, it is important to explore all four voices: both the PROS and CONS of staying where you are on the one hand and the PROS and CONS of changing on the other. It is not enough, for instance, to explore only the pros of changing. It can be tempting to accentuate only the positives for change. If you don't explore the cons of changing and of staying the same these negatives will remain hidden but reappear later and undermine any move towards change. For change to be long-term, people usually need to know how they will deal with the loss as well as enjoy the gain.

Weighing up the Factors

Not all the factors that are explored will have the same weight in the balance. Just to list them or discuss them is not enough.

The effective facilitator is careful not to put their own weighting on the importance of each factor. Rather, by using open questions and reflection the facilitator teases out the relative importance in the other person's world, especially what seems to them important now and what they see as important for the future. By careful summarising, the facilitator can help the other person become more aware of the discrepancy between their current behaviour and what they want for themselves in the future. The motivational balance worksheet S11.1 below has a column where the service user can weight the factors they have listed.

The facilitator's focus remains on exploring, understanding and empathy when building a balance. At some point the other person may say 'I must...', or 'I will have to...', or give other indications that they are beginning to see a direction to move in. These first signs of wishing to be different can be seen as the start of a desire to change. The desire can emerge at any stage, but is often arises when making a motivational balance. Chapter 12 explores how the desire can be nurtured and developed.

On the following pages is a motivational balance that can be copied for personal use and for service users. Some exercises to help with the completion are suggested, but these can be modified to suit the situation and needs of the service user.

Motivational Balance Worksheet S11.1

	MOTIVATIONAL	BALANCE	
Weighting	Reasons I want to stay as I am	Reasons I want to change	Weighting

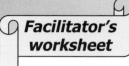

Facilitator's Worksheet F11.1: Exploring Ambivalence Using the Motivational Balance

This is to be used with service user.

Step 1

Agree with the service user an area of behaviour that they are unhappy with, or ambivalent about.

Ask the service user to describe how they would like this part of their life to be different a year from today. Use the *Worksheet S11.2* below if helpful. Your open questions might include:

'Tell me more about how you would like things to be in a years time. Imagine yourself having achieved the change...'

- *What do you see around you in a year's time?*
- *What can you hear others saying to you?*
- *What are you thinking about yourself?*
- *How do you feel?*
- *How much do you really want this goal?*

Step 2. Assess desire to change

Use the worksheet S11.3 below with a service user where helpful.

How much do you want to change? Mark this on the 'I want to' scale.

What is stopping you from standing at 0?

What would need to happen for you to stand one step closer to 10?

Service User's Worksheet S11.2

STEP 1: Describe how you would like your life to be a year from today.
Draw or write key words.

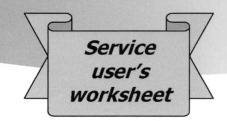

Service user's worksheet

Service User's Worksheet S11.3

Step 2: 'I WANT TO' stepping stones

How much do you want to change?

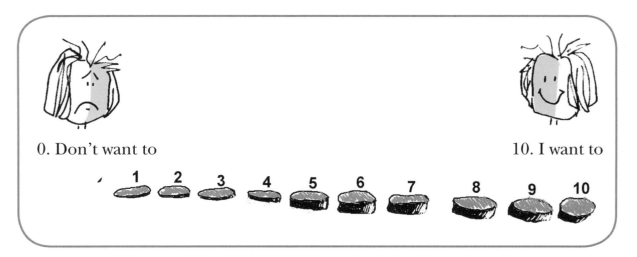

0. Don't want to   10. I want to

1   2   3   4   5   6   7   8   9   10

Imagine the desired change has happened. How does it feel?

Service User's Worksheet S114

Step 3: Motivational balance sheet.

Note reasons in words or pictures why you don't want to change and reasons you do.

MOTIVATIONAL		BALANCE	
Weighting	Reasons I want to stay as I am	Reasons I want to change	Weighting

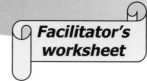

Facilitator's Worksheet F11.2

Step 3: Draw out reasons for change and reasons to stay the same.

Use worksheet S11.4 above

Listen to the reasons given for both changing and staying the same.

The reasons for changing will include what the service user wants for the future and what they do not like about their present situation.

The reasons the service user doesn't want to change will include both what they do not want for the future and want they like about the present situation.

Reflect understanding

Ask the following **Key questions** followed by reflection or silence.

♦ What makes you think what you are doing now could be a problem?

Then draw out concerns with the present behaviour.

♦ In what ways do you think other people may be harmed/ concerned?

♦ What concerns has your girlfriend/boss/courts (or other important people in their life), etc. had?

♦ How do you feel about your behaviour?

♦ In what ways does it concern you?

Key questions to consider the advantages of change

♦ How would changing this behaviour fit with what you really want?

♦ The fact that you're here indicates that part of you wants to change. What are the reasons for change?

♦ What makes you think you need to change?

♦ Tell me how it would make your life better.

Facilitator's Worksheet F11.3

Step 4. Identify core values (see worksheet F11.4 below as an example of how to put core values on the motivational balance sheet).

Ask the service user:

Out of all the reasons given to change or not to change which are the strongest?

Weighting can be added to the decisional balance (worksheet S11.4) by, for instance, adding larger arrows for reasons that are pulling the service user more towards or away from change.

Key questions to draw out core values (weighting):

♦ What are the greatest reasons for change?
♦ What are the greatest reasons for staying the same?

For some service users just doing these exercises will start to raise doubt and initiate change. Self-motivating statements by the service user provide an indication of how desire to change is developing. For example:

'This could be a problem.'
'My partner is concerned about my drinking.'
'I am concerned about my drinking.'
'I need to change'.
'I want to change.'

For others you will find that more time is needed. Where strong reasons to stay the same remain this may be connected with confidence to change. Reframing the reasons given can help to clarify if this is the case and lead into work on confidence building.

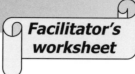

Facilitator's Worksheet F11.4

Example for Step 4.

WHICH REASONS ARE MOST IMPORTANT TO YOU?

Put arrows next to your reasons above. The more important the reason, the bigger the arrow, as exampled below.

	MOTIVATIONAL	BALANCE	
Weighting	**Reasons I want to stay as I am**	**Reasons I want to change**	**Weighting**
←	Have a laugh Meet lots of people	Health	
			→
	What else would I do? Helps me forget worries Easier	£ Keep my partner Pay off debts Job	→ →

SUMMARY

A joy-pain ambivalence is often present where people who are contemplating change cannot yet move on. The motivational balance, when used with the skills of affirmation, listening, reflection and open questions, can help service users to focus on what they really want and what it might cost them to achieve their goal. The next chapter is called 'developing the desire to change' and focuses on managing the cost as well as building the desire to be different.

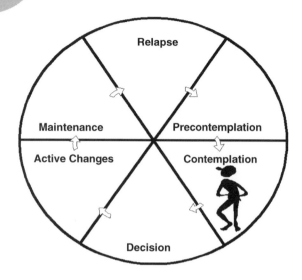

'If you want to move someone it has to be towards a vision which is positive to them.'

Martin Luther King

Chapter 11 began to unpack ambivalence using the motivational balance as a tool. This chapter suggests how to continue that work and draw out the service user's own desires to change.

The skills of affirming, listening and asking open questions are key to enabling the service user to explore their behaviour, thoughts and feelings openly. Without clear goals, however, there is a risk that this is where the work will stay.

The fourth skill, developing discrepancy, is how the facilitator can maintain a clear goal to confront present behaviour whilst using a motivational style. Confrontation becomes the goal not the style. The style includes clear targets of developing discrepancy and drawing out self-motivating statements leading to commitment and confidence in changing behaviour.

DEVELOPING DISCREPANCY

According to the Oxford dictionary 'discrepant' means 'inconsistent'. The object of developing discrepancy is to help service users identify aspects of their current behaviour, which are inconsistent with their core values and beliefs. The skill is to help them realise that the consequences of their current behaviour is likely to be inconsistent with what they say want in the long term; to help them to identify that where they are now is not where they want to be.

If you can think of a pattern of behaviour you have changed yourself there is likely to have been a point where you recognised a discrepancy between current behaviour and longer term goals or values. Examples that have been shared on the courses we have run include:

- A man identifying a discrepancy between his smoking and his desire to marry a woman when she said she loved him but couldn't stand the taste of smoke.
- A woman losing her employment for the third time recognising a discrepancy between her use of alcohol to relax and the disruption it was causing her.
- A man working long hours to provide for his family being asked by his children why he never plays with them.

The aim of motivational interviewing is to aid this natural process by drawing out recognition of inconsistencies that already exist, albeit sometimes hidden.

Self-Motivating Statements

'We know what we believe when we say it ourselves.'

When service users begin to see for themselves the discrepancy between what they do now and what they really want, their unease can be voiced in many forms. The facilitator listens out for these intimations of change and responds by gently enabling service users to explore emerging concerns. Early intimations of change can be delicate states that are easily driven away by enthusiastic affirmation or a plunge into plans for change.

Miller and Rollnick (1991, 2002) first called these utterances 'Self-motivating statements', and later described them as 'change talk'. Self-motivating statements can be heard as the service user gradually voices discomfort with their present state or voices readiness to change.

For example, 'I am not sure I can go on like this' may be slipped in along with other statements. The facilitator might follow up this unease by a simple reflection, inviting the service user to say more about their concern. A range of 'self-motivating statements' is discussed below with some helpful facilitator responses.

Some Self-motivational Statements

STEPS TOWARDS CHANGE

Step 1 - Problem Recognition

'It isn't that they can't see the solution. It is that they can't see the problem.'

G.K. Chesterton

Recognition of a problem is an essential first step. Where the facilitator tries to provide solutions, prior to a shared definition of a problem, resistance is likely to occur. The facilitator needs to draw out a discrepancy between present behaviour and a future goal, for example 'I'm beginning to see that alcohol is causing me some problems'.

Initially there is likely to be some ambivalence about wanting to solve this problem. Ambivalence is the first step towards change.

Step 2 - Concerns

A discrepancy is developed between the belief that the destructive behaviour only has benefits and the evidence to the contrary. Service users start to voice concerns with their behaviour as well as benefits. At first this may be other people's concerns and then gradually they realise they have their own concerns, for example, 'I am concerned about the effect alcohol is having on my relationship with my partner'.

Step 3 – Intention to Change (Commitment Language)

A discrepancy is developed further when the benefits of the current behaviour are seen to outweigh any expressed concerns. The first step may be to say, 'I should do something about this' (Need). The statements become more motivational as the service user says: 'I want to do something about this' (Desire), 'I want to because', (Reasons) and finally 'I will do something about this' (Commitment).

Step 4 – Optimism about Change (Commitment Language)

Where there is a belief that change is not possible, evidence to the contrary is drawn out and highlighted. The facilitator may encourage service users to explore their previous success and build optimism about change this time.

Service users confirm to themselves that they are ready, willing and able to change when they feel comfortable saying:

> 'I want to do it, I can do it and I will start now.'

Amrhein's (2003) found that the more commitment language such as this increased in intensity in the interviews the more likely someone was to change.

See **Chapter 13** for more on optimism about change

APPLYING THE SKILLS
Affirming

The facilitator gives specific praise for desired behaviour and self-motivating statements as they occur.

Listening to the Whole

The facilitator notices body language, which indicates a discomfort with the status quo and hears self-motivating statements and discussion of change.

Reflections

When the service user makes a self-motivating statement, the facilitator follows this up with reflecting the meaning of this statement. The service user's motivation to change increases as they hear their own words repeated and as they add to these. The facilitator can also reflect and summarise visually by drawing a motivational balance. For service users with a strong visual learning preference it can be very helpful to *see* the reasons for and against change when trying to resolve ambivalence.

Reflections and summarising, as we have seen, are also important for breaking up questions leading to a gentler, less confrontational style. Skilful facilitators can conduct a whole interview using only reflections. Even short dialogues that focus on reflecting inconsistencies can be effective.

Evocative Open Questions

Miller and Rollnick (2002) also found that key '*evocative questions*', when used in combination with reflective listening and at the appropriate stage of change, helped to *evoke*, or draw out, self-motivating statements. The statements might be about problem recognition, concerns about current behaviour, intention to change or confidence to change.

Questions that evoke problem recognition include:

- *What problems is alcohol causing you?*
- *What is the biggest problem?*
- *How would you like your life to be different in a year's time?*

Questions that evoke concern include:

- *What concerns you about alcohol?*
- *What are the disadvantages of taking alcohol?*

Questions which evoke intention to change include:

- *What were the good things about changing when you did it before?*
- *What are the benefits of changing?*
- *What makes you feel it is important to change?*
- *What makes you feel you will change?*

Questions which evoke optimism include:

- *If you could do it which of your skills would you use?*
- *What makes your partner think you can do it?*
- *On a scale from 0–10 how confident are you that you could make a start?*
- *What stops you standing at 0?*

The art to using the Socratic and evocative questions successfully is to listen and hear the appropriate time to nudge the service user forward and then follow up with reflections.

Avoid suggestions disguised as questions, such as:

- Why don't you just ask why?
- Why don't you leave him?
- Why don't you just stop going to that pub?

These are similar to the 'Have you thought about …?' questions.

If the reaction is 'ah but…' the facilitator will know that a suggestion has been made too early and resistance is likely to be reinforced by continuing.

Example Interview

The interview below provides an example of how the motivational skills of exploring ambivalence and developing desire to change can be combined to draw out self-motivating statements to initiate change.

Facilitator:	**Welcome Carol, I am glad you managed to find the office. We spoke on the phone last week and you mentioned that your doctor had referred you to me in relation to your smoking. We have half an hour today which you can use to talk about anything you want to. Everything is confidential to the meeting and we can meet again if that is helpful to you. [Contracting] What else would you like to ask me before we begin? [Open question giving control to Carol]**
Carol:	Nothing really. It's my doctor who thinks I should smoke less. I don't know why I'm here really. It's taken me all morning to

get here and it's up to me whether I stop or not. I'm not even sure if I want to anyway. Nothing you can say can make any difference to that. *[Ambivalence and some resistance to change]*

Facilitator: **I get the impression that coming here has been a big step for you and you feel anxious about whether anything will change. [*Reflection of feelings*]**

Carol: Yes, it has been a big step for me. The doctor said if I didn't stop smoking I wouldn't be around in a year's time, but then if I am going to die, I might as well die happy.

Facilitator: **So, on the one hand you wonder whether changing your behaviour will make any difference to how long you live and on the other you have made quite a big effort to get here to talk about it. [*Reflection of ambivalence/ developing discrepancy*]**

Carol: Well, I do enjoy smoking. It helps me forget my problems and relax when I get stressed, and once you have been smoking as long as I have it might do more harm than good to stop. *[Benefits of staying the same]*

Facilitator: **So you are thinking you may as well carry on, and you doubt whether there are benefits to stopping. [*Amplified reflection of meaning/developing discrepancy*]**

Carol: Mind you most of my problems and worries are about my health and if I stopped smoking I might not worry about them so much. The doctor says I wouldn't have had to have the operations if I hadn't smoked and she thinks if I stop I could really improve my life chances. It's probably too late though, I might as well enjoy life?

Facilitator: **So your doctor feels that if you stopped smoking your health and life expectancy are likely to improve , but you wonder if this is correct and also if you could enjoy life if you didn't smoke. [*Reflection/developing discrepancy*]**

Carol:	Well, she is probably right. I could enjoy life if I didn't smoke. It's short term that it would be a right hassle. I've failed three times before. The longest I have given up is for six months.
Facilitator:	**It's interesting that you have seriously thought about stopping before and successfully achieved this for quite a long time. What made it seem important enough for you to make this effort?** *[Reframing and Socratic question]*
Carol:	I wanted to be healthier, not to run out of breath all the time.
Facilitator:	**When you stopped smoking how did it affect you?** *[Evocative question drawing out positives of not smoking]*
Carol:	I could run for the bus. I didn't run out of breath when I climbed the stairs. My clothes were cleaner and breath smelt better, and I didn't worry about the effect on the children.
Facilitator:	**(Nods)**
Carol:	My partner and kids were much happier too. I think they were proud of me for once.
Facilitator:	**So your health on a day-to-day basis felt better and you were getting on better with your family, as well as feeling better about your appearance. You were smiling when you described this as if it was a time you felt good.** *[Summarising]*
Carol:	Yes, I was feeling much better. Until I was told I needed the operations and then I started again, even though the doctor told me it would be the worst thing to do and once I started I needed to carry on to stop myself worrying what would happen to me.
Facilitator:	**Being without cigarettes long term relaxes you, but short-term smoking seems to be a quick fix.** *[Summary of ambivalence]*

> *Carol:*   I need to smoke to relax, but longer term I want to stop smoking. Smoking doesn't solve anything for me, it just makes things worse. *[Self-motivational statement]*
>
> **Facilitator:**   **How much on a scale from nought to 10 do you want to stop smoking?** *[Exploring motivation]*
>
> *Carol:*   A six. There are quite a few reasons really why I want to stop largely to do with my health, but I also enjoy it. It's confusing!

The interview goes on to use the motivational balance as a framework to help unravel this confusion, and this is summarised below.

Carol's motivational balance

Weighting	Reasons I want to stay as I am	Reasons I want to change	Weighting
	Short term	**Short term**	
Medium	Enjoy the company of others who smoke	Don't like the smell on clothes	Low
Medium	Trigger for end of the day	Children don't like it	Medium
Low	Something to do with my hands	Arguments with partner	High
		Long term	
High	Hard to change	Health- I don't want another operation	High
High	Helps me relax	I want to be able to move around easily/enjoy life	High
High	Need the 'fix'	Being around for the children as they grow up	High
	Long term		
	None		

Facilitator: *What do you think is the biggest reason you want to stop?* *[Evocative question]*

Carol: My health…I'm worried that if I don't stop I won't be around in another year and what will the children do without me?

Facilitator: **Your children are very important to you.** *[Reflection to focus interview on importance of children]*

Carol: They are both wonderful kids. They mean the world to me.

Facilitator: **They are your world.** *[Reflection]* **What do you think you mean to them?** *[Socratic question]*

Carol: I'm their mum, we have fun together, but they rely on me. They are still so young; Sam is six and Jade is 10.

Facilitator: **So in the year's time your doctor mentioned, they will be seven and 11. Imagine that year has passed and your health has improved in the way your doctor says it could. What can you see happening in your life?** *[Imagining a future goal]*

Carol: Jade will be going to secondary school. I can just see her in that smart uniform on her first day.

Facilitator: **You seem very proud of her.** *[Reflection of feeling]* **What would you really like to hear her saying to you when she comes back?** *[Evocative question about her future wants]*

Carol: How pleased she is that I am around to take her to the bus and hear the excitement of everything which has happened in the day.

Facilitator. **It sounds like a really important day for her, which you would very much want to be part of.** *[Reflection of meaning]*

Carol: Yes, I would like to give her a kiss, tell her I love her and how proud I am of her.

Facilitator: **How will that make you feel?**

Carol: That it has all been worth it…Yes, it's the children which are the biggest reason I want to stop smoking. I want to be there for them. It's not a 6, it's more than that. *[Stronger self-motivational statement. Notice this reason was not apparent at the start of the interview]*

Facilitator: **Your children seem to be very important to you and it sounds like thinking of them helps you to want to live a healthier lifestyle.** *[Reflection of meaning]*

Carol: Yes, I want to be healthier and to be around for them in a year and for many years after that, it's just that in the short term I feel so much better when I have a cigarette.

Facilitator: **So your biggest reasons for staying the same are that it helps you relax, you feel you need it and it's difficult to change. Your biggest reasons to change are your children, your health and a better relationship with your partner. Overall you have given most weight to being with your children. In the short term you find smoking relaxes you and helps reduce your anxiety.** *[Summary of motivational balance]*

Carol: When I hear myself say it, there is no contest. I just need to believe that I can do it and relax in some other way.

Facilitator: **So feeling able to change and having alternatives are areas you would like to develop. (Carol nods) Imagine you are standing at 10 for wanting to change and you have no doubts that this is the way forward for you … What are you saying to yourself?** *[Imaging a future goal]*

Carol: It's my choice; I am the only person who can make sure I'm there for my kids. *[Self-motivational statement]*

Facilitator: **I noticed that you were sitting much more erect when you said that and your voice was stronger.** [*Reflection of body language and voice*]

Carol: Yes, it's strange that being clearer about what I want helps me to think it is possible. [*Self-motivating statement*]

Facilitator: **I am impressed by your determination for what you really, really want as a mother.** [*Affirmation*]

Interview ends with a summary, agreement to focus on building confidence next time and the facilitator asking Carol when she would like to meet again.

Carol: I would like to meet in fortnight if that is alright and see if I can stop smoking for that length of time. [Ending on a self-motivating statement]

You can read about the second meeting with Carol in Chapter 13.

Facilitator's Worksheet F12.1: I Want to ...

Use the worksheets below to help service users identify and prioritise areas of their behaviour that they want to change.

S12.1 Use to draw out key positive values and help service user's identify current behaviour which conflicts with these values as well as positive behaviour they want to continue.

S12.2 Use to help service users set and refine goals. Change the date for achieving the goal to suit the service user.

S12.3 Use to help service users prioritise goals.

S.12.4 Use to draw out commitment language.

- Need to change – 'I am concerned about my behaviour and need to change.'
- Desire to change – 'I want to change.'
- Reasons to change – 'I want to change because…'
- Ability to change – 'I can change because…'
- Commitment to change – 'I will change.'

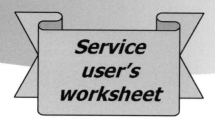

Service User's Worksheet S12.1: Who I am and Who I want to Become

Use this sheet to work out your main values, behaviour which supports these values and behaviour which does not.

Values It is important for me to be…	Behaviour which fits with my values I like myself when I…	Behaviour which does not fit with my values I dislike myself when I…
Example Trusted by others	Do what I have said I will	Steal something

Service User's Worksheet S12.2: What do I want to change?

1. Write below the main things you would like to achieve in the next year.
2. Image what it will look like, feel and sound like if you get each of your goals.
3. How will it affect people you care about?
4. Cross off anything you don't really want.
5. Cross off anything outside of your control.
6. Cross off anything which does not fit with the sort of person you are and want to be. (See S12.1)

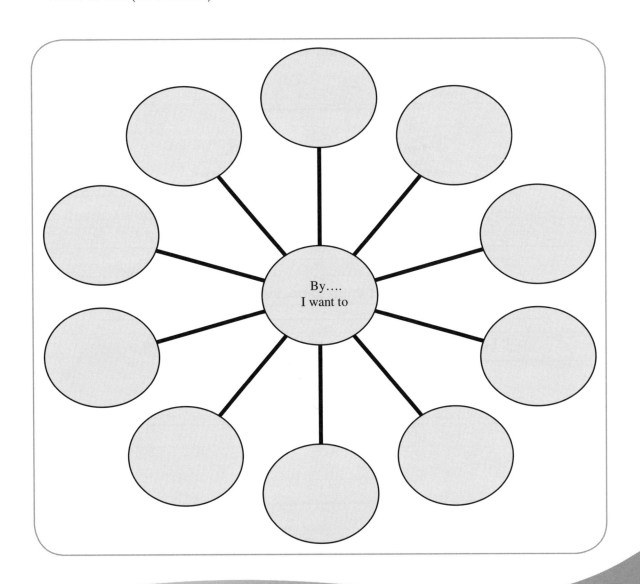

By....
I want to

Service User's Worksheet S12.3: Source of motivation

Which of your goals meet the
higher levels of the pyramid below?

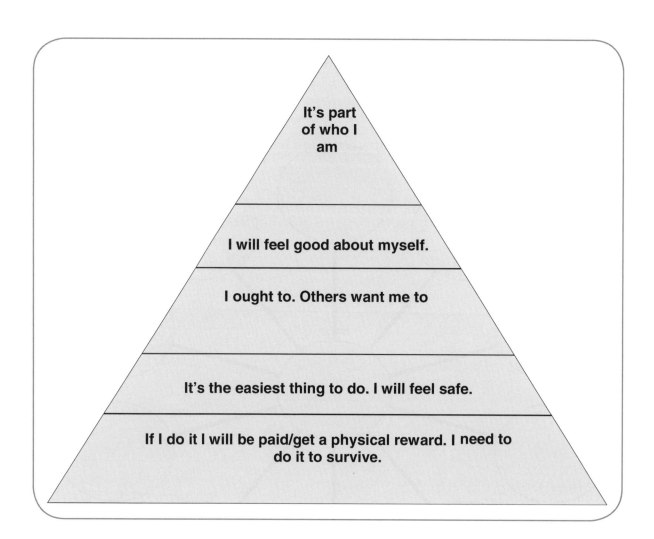

It's part
of who I
am

I will feel good about myself.

I ought to. Others want me to

It's the easiest thing to do. I will feel safe.

If I do it I will be paid/get a physical reward. I need to
do it to survive.

Service
user's
worksheet

Service User's Worksheet
S12.4: I Want to

Identify one goal that fits with your values
and the higher levels of the pyramid.
Mark on the line below how much you really
want to achieve this goal (0 is low and 10 is
high).

0…..1…..2…..3…..4…..5…..6…..7…..8…..9…..10
Don't want to   **Really want to**

1. What concerns you about your present behaviour?

2. What is the biggest reason for you making the change?

3. What makes you think you can change?

4. What makes you think you will change?

SUMMARY

The service user's desire to change often arises from their awareness of the discrepancy between their current behaviour and what they really want. For the desire to be translated into action requires the service user to have some confidence in their ability to change. This is the subject of the next chapter called 'affirmation and confidence to change.'

Chapter

13

> 'If you treat a man as he is , he will stay as he is, but if you treat him as if he were what he could be, he will become what could be.'
>
> *Johann Wolfgang Von Goethe*

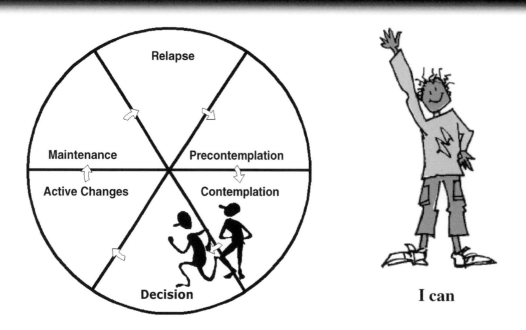

I can

BUILDING CONFIDENCE

If you think about your own life there may be some areas which you really want to change, but doubt that you can. What happens if your doubts grow? Unless you are very determined, you may find that you doubt you really wanted to change in the first place. What happens if you become more confident about your ability to change? You may well find that your desire to change gets greater and that you are much more likely to take the first step. This is a common 'rationalising experience'.

As a facilitator of change it is crucial to hear and see moments when the desire to change is high but confidence still needs to be built. Your focus as a facilitator then moves from building desire to 'affirmation'.

AFFIRMATION

A motivational approach affirms in two ways. Firstly, individuals voice for themselves their own belief in the possibility of change. Secondly, the facilitator reflects back evidence of ability to change. The emphasis is on the facilitator asking questions which help the service user voice for themselves their own strengths: evocative questions. For instance, the facilitator might ask, 'Tell me some of your skills you will use when you do change.' The question focuses

the service user on their positive strengths. The impact of the service user naming these strengths is very different from the facilitator simply saying, 'You can do it.'

This is not to say that as a facilitator of change you do not demonstrate your own confidence in the service user's ability to change; indeed there is research evidence to suggest that it is important to do so. As a facilitator of change you will make many positive statements when you reflect what is seen and heard, for instance, the facilitator might say:

> 'You mentioned earlier that you successfully controlled your diabetes for three months and that you planned your diet with your partner.'

or

> 'I noticed you always arrive on time for your appointments. It seems to me that you have skills in managing your time.'

Again, if you think about your own experience, how do you feel about yourself when someone listens to everything you say with interest? What sort of non-verbal communication makes you doubt your own ability and what sort of non-verbal communication strengthens it? Reflective listening, rapport and positive non-verbal communication are all part of affirmation and help to build confidence to change.

For some service users the initial period of contact with your agency can be a kind of 'honeymoon' period when there is a window of opportunity to build motivation. Desire to change can be quite high at this stage particularly where the service user has referred themselves. Building confidence at this stage can prevent a later drop in motivation.

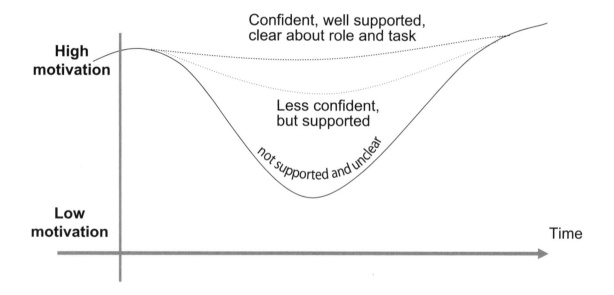

The above diagram illustrates how motivation dips in nearly any venture, but can recover as confidence is built. Often people enter into a task with a high motivation to 'do something about it this time'. As they encounter the difficulties to be overcome, they may feel daunted. Motivation drops as confidence evaporates. A focus on building confidence can then help restore motivation.

The affirmation exercises that follow can be used with service users to help them explore and increase their current levels of confidence to change. Adapt the exercises to suit the people you are working with. As you discuss the exercises listen to the service user's ideas and concerns, observe and affirm body language. Reflect back any self-motivating statements and encourage service users to tell you more. Be guided by the service user rather than sticking rigidly to the exercises.

Service User's Worksheet S13.1:

Building Confidence - Step 1

1. What is the behaviour you want to change?

2. Mark with a cross on the ladder below how confident you are about changing (10 is confident, 0 is not confident).

I can

10

5

0

I can't

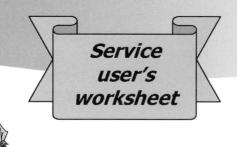

Service User's Worksheet S13.2:
Building Confidence - Step 2

1. What stops you standing at 0 on the ladder?

2. What would need to happen for you to take another step towards 10?

Imagine you are standing at 10.

3. What helped you to get there?

4. Who else helped you?

Service user's worksheet

Service User's Worksheet S13.3:

**Step 3 - Identify Below Some Things
That You Can Do Now**

---

1. Include the skills you use to cope with everyday situations.

I can:

2. Include the skills you used when you did something well.

I can:

3. Include what other people say you can do.

I can:

S13.3 continued...

Write down the things you can do well now.

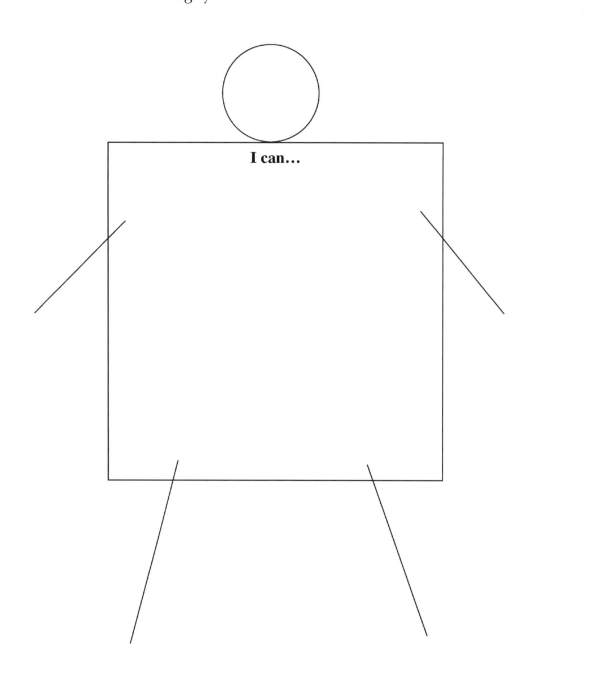

I can...

Which of these skills could you use to help you take another step towards 10 on the 'I can' ladder?

Service user's worksheet

Service User's Worksheet S13.4:

Step 4 - What Gets in the Way?

In the table below write down:,

1. What gets in the way?	2. If I was able to change, I would ...
Who does not help you?	

Service User's Worksheet S13.5:

Step 5 - Who can Help?

Identify on the chart below all the people you know who can help you change.

- Who has helped you before?
- Who believes you can do it?
- Who will be most pleased if you do change?

Imagine you have changed.

- Who helped you most?

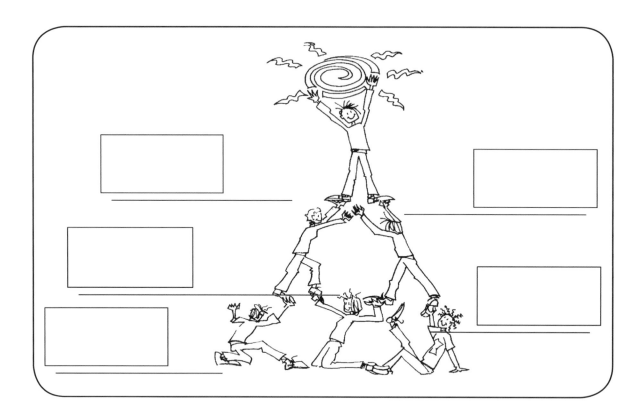

Service User's Worksheet S13.6:

Step 6 - A Little Help from your Friends

1. What do you hear other people say that helps you to change?

2. What have other people said you are good at?

3. Imagine you have changed. What do you hear other people saying?

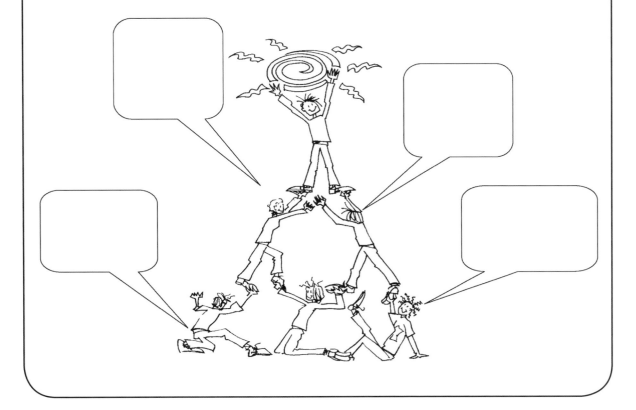

Service User's Worksheet S13.7:

Step 7 - Looking Back 1

Remember times when you were your own worst enemy.

1. What did you do and say?

2. What did you think?

3. How do you feel?

Service User's Worksheet S13.8:

Step 8 - Looking Back 2

Remember the times you were your own best friend; when you thought you couldn't change but you did, a time when you did well, a time when you felt good about yourself.

What were the strengths you used?

Service User's Worksheet S13.9:

Step 9 - Other Options

Think back to when you were your own worst enemy.

What other things could you have done?

What else could you have said?

How would you have felt as a result?

Service User's Worksheet S13.10:

Step 10 - Overcoming Barriers

Go back to your barriers to change worksheet (S13.4). What can you do to overcome your barriers?

I can

Who can help you?

A Motivational Interview with Carol - Building Confidence

(See the start of this interview with Carol in Chapter 12.)

Facilitator: **Welcome, Carol. It is good to see you again. It has been two weeks since you first saw me. You have explored the reasons you want to stop smoking as well as what you are getting from it. On the last occasion your desire to live a healthier life style came over as quite strong particularly in terms of improving your chances of being able to physically do things and to support your children You indicated last time that you wanted to explore further how you can do this. [*Contracting and summary*]**

Carol: Yes, I have decided that I definitely want to stop smoking. I have made an effort to do this and it worked for a short period of time. I managed to go two days without a cigarette at all, after our first meeting and I thought for a moment that that was it, that I had cracked it, but here I am again still smoking. I have cut down but not as much as I would like to.

Facilitator: **You sounded as if you were standing at the '10' in terms of wanting to change. [*Reflection*]**

Carol: Yes it was the thought of the operation and the children. I, just repeated to myself what I really wanted, which helped enormously, but then I gradually started again. Perhaps I'm just addicted and can't change.

Facilitator: **On the one hand you wonder if you can change your behaviour and on the other you are aware that you have already made some steps towards this. You stopped for two full days and have stopped for up to six months in the past. [*Reflection of ambivalence/developing discrepancy*]**

Carol: Yes, I can do it if I think about the children and use the plastic cigarettes whenever I desperately wanted to smoke. It's just when I get home from work and feel tired and stressed.

Facilitator:	**When you get home from work is a really risk time for you. [*Reflection*]**
Carol:	As soon as I get in I start talking with the child minder who smokes and always offers me one. It's so much easier to say 'yes' and think it will only be one, only it usually ends up being two or three.
Facilitator:	**You find it difficult to tell people you are no longer smoking when they offer you a cigarette. [*Reflection of meaning*]**
Carol:	Yes, when it's the end of the day and when I am with other people who smoke; especially friends. I'm ok when I am at work, with my partner or the children. I can keep my mind off it.
Facilitator:	**You only smoke when you are with other people who smoke. [*Amplified reflection*]**
Carol:	Well I also smoke after someone has moaned at me. My partner gets really annoyed about it at times which makes me feel so useless and smoking helps calm me down.

The interview continues with the facilitator drawing out the situations where Carol smokes and when she manages to control her smoking. The first part of the 'What gets in the way?' exercise (see service user's worksheet S13.4, above) is completed and discussed.

Carol's Completed 'What gets in the way?'

Exercise (Worksheet S13.4)

What gets in the way?	If I was able to change, I would...
Need to relax when I get home	Do something else to relax
Child minder is smoking	Ask her not to smoke or get another child minder
Offered a cigarette	Say 'no'
Enjoy going out with friends to the pub and then I smoke	Go out with other friends. Stay with those who don't smoke and find out what they do
After an argument I go to my friend, moan and smoke	Sort out my relationship with my partner so we argued less.
Who does not help you?	Child minder
	Work mates who smoke
	Partner when he criticises me

Carol also completed the worksheet S13.5 step 5 'Who can help'. The two exercises and discussions helped Carol to work out the three main areas of support she wanted, namely from her partner, from others in a similar situation and to have a smoke-free environment at home.

> *Facilitator:* **I'd like you to imagine for a minute: that you have got the main support you want: that your home is always free of others smoking: that you can talk with someone who doesn't smoke when you are anxious or very tempted to smoke: that you and you partner praise each other for achievements more than you criticise each other: ...**
>
> **Which of these did you imagine you achieved first?**
>
> [*Socratic question*]

Carol:	Getting someone to talk to when I am tempted to smoke.
Facilitator:	**You sound pretty confident about that.** [*Reflection of Carol's voice tone and demeanour*]
Carol:	Yes, I was put in touch with a group by my doctor that I could join and which worked really well for me last time I gave up smoking. I could join that again and could phone people whenever I needed a chat.
Facilitator:	**So joining the support group would be an achievable first step.** [*Reflection of confidence*]
Carol:	I would also like to think about making my home smoke free but I know that would take more of an effort and it would help if my partner and I did this together. I'm not sure how I would tell the child minder to stop smoking.
Facilitator:	**You say it's so important for you to come home to a place where there is no one smoking and to involve your partner more.** [*Reflection of desired outcome*]
Carol:	Yes, I think the best option would probably be to talk to my partner first and let him know how difficult it is for me.
Facilitator:	**How confident are you on a scale from 0-10 that you will talk with him about the childminder and others smoking?**
Carol:	Nine
Facilitator:	**What would make it 10?** [*Evocative question to draw out self-motivating statement*]
Carol:	Just deciding when I will do it. I will need to make sure we are both in the right mood and no one else is around. Just after the children have gone to bed sounds like a good time.

> *Facilitator:* **And you said earlier that you wanted to praise each other rather than criticise.** [*Reflection of previous self-motivating statement*]
>
> *Carol:* Yes I could start with something I am pleased about and perhaps he would be more likely to be pleased with me.
>
> *Facilitator:* **It sounds like you have a number of ideas on how to get a more supportive environment for you to change. Remind me what steps you are going to take before we meet again.** [*Evocative question*]
>
> *Carol:* I am going to rejoin the support group which helped me before. I am going to make the first step towards a smoke free home and I am going to take the step toward a better relationship with my partner by telling him what a good cook he is. I'm also not going to smoke for the rest of the day. [*Commitment talk*]

SUMMARY

Motivational affirmation focuses on empowerment. The service user is encouraged to draw out their own resources and to believe in the possibility of change. Chapter 14 will explore how to put this belief into action.

> *'Whether you believe you can or whether you believe you cannot; you are probably right.'*
>
> *Henry Ford*

Motivational Action Planning

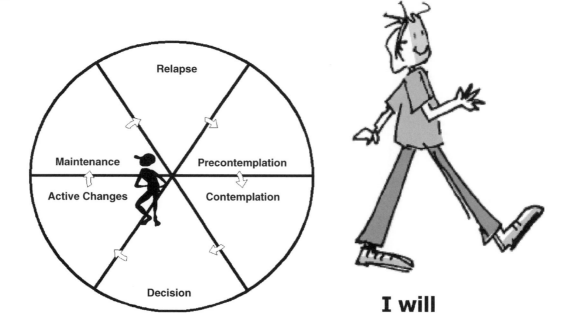

I will

> 'If you don't know where you are going you are likely to end up somewhere else.'
>
> *Laurence J. Peter*

Planning how to achieve a change works best once someone has fully decided that they want to change. Although this sounds obvious, practice can be very different. As soon as there is any sign of a problem, the pressure is on the facilitator to plan how to 'fix' it. The pressure may arise from your wish to do something for the service user, or from the agency's requirement to produce an action plan. The temptation is to assume that any sign of readiness to change indicates a full commitment to change, and a rush into solutions. A motivational approach will first establish what a service user is ready to change and then empower them to take responsibility for how that change will happen.

Chapter 14 will explore:

1. How to recognise readiness for change.
2. How to set goals and strengthen commitment to change.
3. Motivational action planning.

SIGNS OF READINESS TO CHANGE

The area the service user is ready to consider changing may not be the same as the one the facilitator was targeting, but they may both lead to the same ultimate goal. A service user, for instance, may not yet want to reduce their alcohol intake, but might want to:

♦ gain employment
♦ improve health
♦ reduce offending.

A genuine expression of desire to change is a window of opportunity for the facilitator. It can sometimes be helpful to start with the service user's agenda and link it at a later stage with your own and the agency's agenda. If the facilitator continues to explore desire to change, rather than moving onto building confidence and commitment, this opportunity can be lost. Motivational skills of listening and open questions will continue to be useful, but the previous emphasis on summarising starts to reduce. The principle of developing self-belief in change starts to have a greater emphasis than the principle of developing discrepancy. Additional skills of negotiating goals and action planning are needed.

The art of a motivational approach is to recognise the right time to shift focus. The focus might be on action plans and then move back to contemplation for a while, and then on to building confidence. The change in focus will ideally be smooth, effortless and natural. The change facilitator's exercise below can be used as a check list to help you identify if the time has arrived to start to shift your focus.

Commitment Language - Some Clues to Lookout For

'Until one is committed there is hesitancy ... Once someone is fully committed all sorts of things occur to help one that would never otherwise have occurred. A whole stream of events issue from the decision.'

Johann Wolfgang Von Goethe

A service user who really wants to change and feels some confidence in change will demonstrate this in both their verbal and non-verbal language.

Language that *implies someone* else wants them to change, such as:

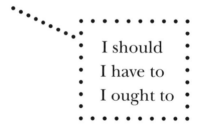

I should

I have to

I ought to

is replaced with language that implies a strong *personal desire to change*, such as:

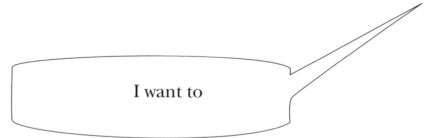

I want to

Language that implies a *limited self-belief*, such as:

I will try

I don't know if I can

I would if I could

is replaced with language that implies *confidence and self-responsibility*, such as:

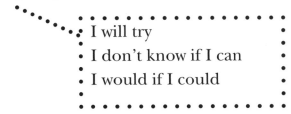

One thing I can do is…

I can do it

Language that implies *hesitancy*, such as:

I might

I will sometime

is replaced with language that implies *certainty*, such as:

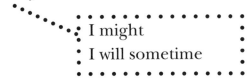

I will do this today

Body language and tone of voice will support the verbal language when the desire to change is genuine. Although there are cultural and gender differences, someone who is committed to change is generally more likely to maintain eye contact, express the feeling they are talking about with their face, body and tone of voice. Often you will notice that the anxiety or depression which was expressed at the contemplation stage starts to lift and is replaced with more peaceful, relaxed body language. Where there is incongruence, where the verbal language says one thing and the body language another, it is generally safest to believe the body language.

Facilitator's Worksheet F14.1:
Signs of Commitment to Change

Use this checklist to help you evaluate whether it is appropriate to move on to goal setting and action planning.

The service user is expressing:

- ☐ Self-motivating statements over a period of time - 'This is a problem', I *want* to change', 'I *can* change', 'I *will* change'.

- ☐ Increased strength of commitment to change in conversation, including a strong *desire* to change, *ability* to change, reasons to change and *need* to change.

- ☐ Clear links between short-term and longer term goals and values.

- ☐ A vision of a future with the changed behaviour as central to it.

- ☐ Self-responsibility for change.

- ☐ Confidence in their own strengths and how to overcome some barriers.

- ☐ Self-belief in change.

- ☐ The desire to change increasingly over a period of time, rather than suddenly.

- ☐ Descriptions of small steps towards change.

Goal Setting

> Alice: 'Would you tell me, please, which way I ought to go from here?' The
>
> Cat: 'That depends a good deal on where you want to get to.'
>
> Lewis Carroll, *Alice in Wonderland* (1866).

Once a clear decision to change has been made the next step is to set motivational and achievable goals. A motivational approach does not impose these goals, but instead draws them out from the service user and helps to refine them towards goals which are:

♦ **S**pecific - Have a clear outcome; e.g. 'I want to fit into a size 14', rather than 'I want to lose weight'
♦ **M**easurable - Progress towards the goal can be monitored.
♦ **A**chievable - Something the service user can do
♦ **R**elevant - The goal fits with longer term values and other goals the service user has, and fits with agency goals
♦ **T**ime limited - With a specific date for achievement
♦ **O**wned - Selected by the service user rather than the facilitator
♦ **P**ositive - Framed as something that is wanted, rather than something which is not wanted; e.g. 'I want to obtain and keep employment', rather than 'I don't want to be drunk every morning'.

Where the service users sets goals which are unrealistic , rather than arguing or trying to persuade, you can question and reflects the inconsistencies and develop the services user's own desire to change the goal.

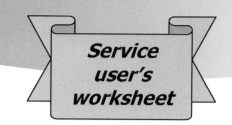

Service User's Worksheet S14.1: Clarifying Outcomes

Write in the space below what you *really* want
to change/do by what date.

Put what you want to do rather than what you don't want to do

By...I will

....

....

Check that this is within your control and change it if it is not

By...I will

....

....

1. What will it look if you do change?

2. What will you hear around you?

3. How will you feel?

4. What will people you care about think about the change?

Service User's Worksheet S14.2

How much do you believe you will change?

On the target below, mark how close to your target you believe you will get.

If you think you won't do anything towards it put a cross in the outer circle (I won't – 0). If you think you might change put a cross half way towards the middle (5)

If you think you definitely will make the full change put a cross in the very middle (I will – 10).

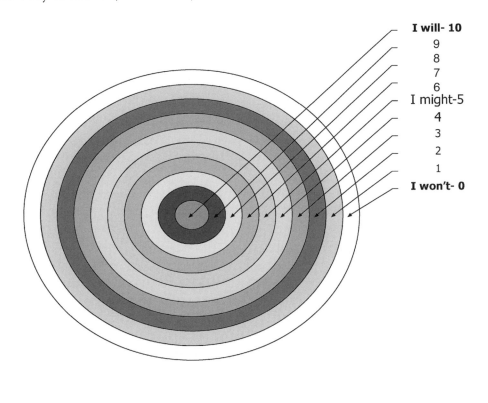

I will- 10
9
8
7
6
I might-5
4
3
2
1
I won't- 0

Planning for Change

> '*If you fail to plan you plan to fail.*'
>
> *Proverb*

There a numerous ways in which a goal can be achieved. Different methods work for different people. Providing only one option invites the service user to say what is wrong with it. A motivational approach aims to draw out a variety of options with the service user and then invites them to select which to work on.

At this stage the quantity of options is more important than the quality. The brain-stimulating process of gathering all the options is as valuable as the option list itself. Options that may at first seem ridiculous or harmful still need to be expressed, so that potentially valuable contributions are not missed. When the service user or the facilitator starts to say:

It can't be done

It would never work

Ask:

- ◆ '*What if...?*' questions
- ◆ '*What if* there was transport provided?*'
- ◆ '*What if* someone helped you?*'
- ◆ '*What if it could be done?*'

As more creative ideas are unleashed a solution to the obstacle may be found or another option generated.

Once the service user has exhausted options and is asking for more ideas, it may be helpful for the facilitator to provide a series of relevant options in language that the service user understands.

Service user's worksheet

Service User's Worksheet S14.3:

Negotiating a Plan – Options

What can I do?

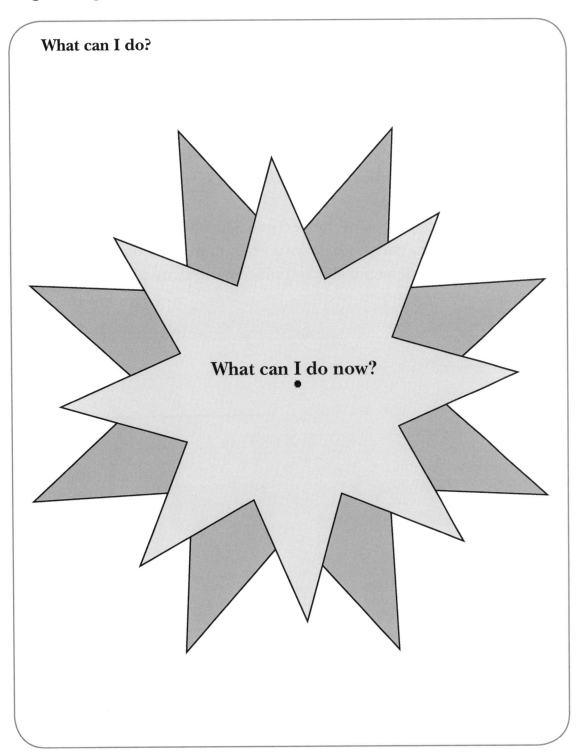

What can I do now?

Selecting an Option

♦ When as many options as possible have been generated, narrow the options down to two or three.

♦ The onus for selection needs to be with the service user if they are going to 'own' the decision rather than blame the facilitator when things go wrong.

♦ What may seem like the best options to you is not always the same for someone else.

♦ Once the options have been narrowed down, encourage questions and discussions of feelings about the options as well as more logical advantages and disadvantages.

♦ Sometimes an adaptation of the decisional balance can be helpful in considering the merits of two options when there is a dilemma.

♦ At other times it will be possible to pursue more than one option at a time.

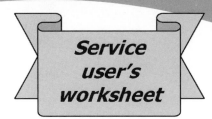

Service User's Worksheet S144:

Negotiating a Plan. Shall I do This or That?

Copy this sheet to consider more than one option.

Option. I could:

....

....

Reasons not to:	Reasons to:

Identifying Smaller Steps

'It is better to take many small steps in the right direction than to make a great leap forward only to stumble backward.'

Chinese proverb

Once an option has been selected it can be helpful to identify smaller steps to achieve it. A motivational approach helps the service user identify these steps for themselves and consider how much they *want* to, *can* and *will* take at each step. Use the exercises below to assist this process.

Service User's Worksheet S14.5:

Negotiating a Plan – First Steps

Identify three steps towards change that you really *want* to take and *can* achieve.

Now rate how confident you are that you *will* make the step.

Change the steps if you rate your commitment less than eight.

Add the date you will do it by.

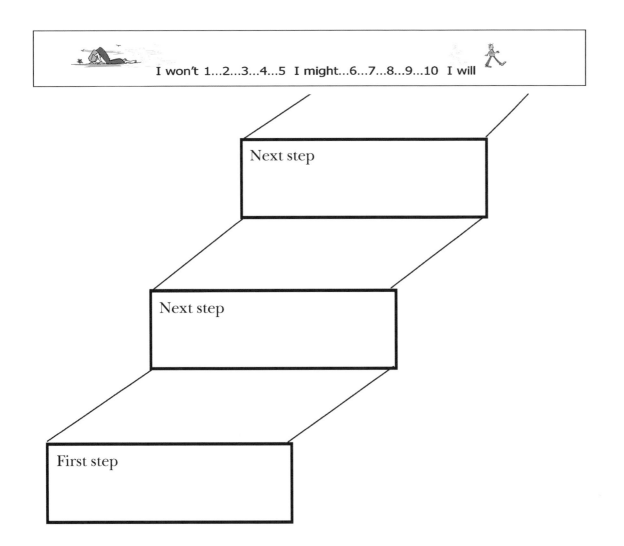

I won't 1...2...3...4...5 I might...6...7...8...9...10 I will

Next step

Next step

First step

Service user's worksheet

Service User's Worksheet S14.6:
Negotiating a Plan – Putting it into Practice

1. Who will I share the plan with?

2. When and how will I record progress?

3. What will I do if I lapse and who will help me?

4. What will I do, think and feel when I have changed?

Summarising the Decision to Change

Once a decision has been finalised it is helpful to revise your contract with the service user to include this decision. It is important to end on a positive note and with a high level of commitment language from the service user. Rather than asking, 'Do you agree with the plan?', which is likely to just produce a 'Yes'. It is helpful in the last few minutes to ask a few key questions to draw out self-motivating statements for change such as:

- 'What have you decided to do?'
- 'How will your life be better when you do change?'
- 'How will you make sure you do it?'

The last question leads you into the issue of how you support someone who has decided to change, which will be explored in Chapter 15.

> 'Whether you believe you will or whether you believe you won't; you are probably right.'

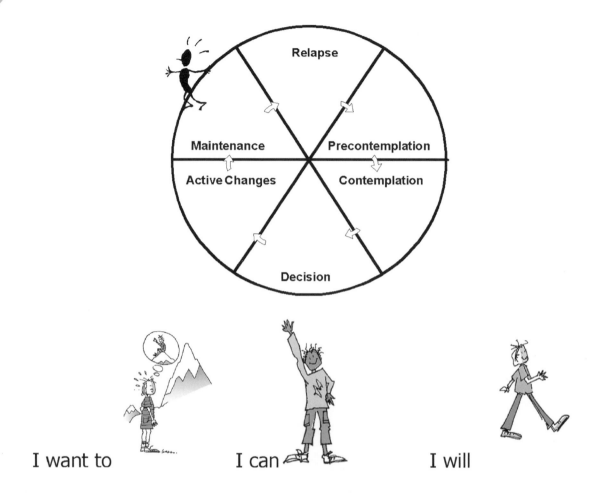

I want to   I can   I will

'A journey of a thousand miles begins with a single step.'

Lao-tzu, The Way of Lao-tzu, Chinese philosopher (604BC–531BC)

Chapter 15 will explore how motivational skills can be used in conjunction with other skills once a firm commitment to change has been made. At the action and maintenance stages of change it is important to move onto developing the confidence and competence to change, so that you hear not only, 'I want to change', but also, 'I can change, I will change, I know how to change, I am changing, and I have changed.'

Develop Confidence to Change Rather than Desire to Change

Miller and Rollnick (2002) refer to the action stage as the start of the downhill slope towards change. The hard climb up the mountain of change has occurred and all that is left is to ski down to the bottom of the slope. For someone who has never skied before, however, the prospect of this downhill run can be frightening. It is not uncommon, for people who have been 'addicted' to behaviour to describe change as the hardest thing they have done in their lives.

A novice skier at this stage no longer needs to focus on building the desire to reach the bottom; indeed this may be counterproductive. Rather they need assistance from someone who is competent, someone who has the skills, knows the route down and can provide feedback on progress.

Building confidence and new skills draws on the same principles as building the desire to change: empathy; avoiding argument; highlighting discrepancies or inconsistencies; building self-responsibility.

Highlight Discrepancies Rather than just Reassure

When a novice skier expresses an inability to change, the motivational ski instructor would both reassure and highlight inconsistencies in the beliefs which act as barriers to change.

Novice skier: 'I can't do it.'

Ski instructor: **'What is your biggest fear?'**

Novice skier: 'That I will forget how to stop.'

Ski instructor: **'Show me what you can do to stop.'**

Instructor then observes, affirms and provides feedback.

Ski instructor: **'If you did feel confident to start which slope would you start on?'**

Empathy

What works for one person will not necessarily work for another. Just as the motivational ski instructor will constantly seek to understand the different fears, experiences and strengths of each novice skier so the facilitator of change will constantly seek to gain a genuine understanding of each individual. The motivational skills of listening, observing, open questions, and summarising understanding, are essential to gain empathy and respond to individual need.

Avoid Argument

Teaching new behaviours and tips on how to change can work well at the action stage. The novice skier, for instance, wants to know exactly what to do. However, should you hear resistance and reasons not to take up advice, this is an indication to change tack. Focus on listening to fears and anxieties, build confidence and provide choices rather than solutions.

Support Self-belief and Self-responsibility

Confidence, self-belief and new skills are the keys to reach the bottom of the mountain and leave the cycle of change altogether. Use the exercise F15.1 to reflect and plan how you will build on your own practice for the future.

Facilitator's worksheet

Facilitator's Worksheet F15.1: Supporting First Steps Towards Change

Identify a service user who is starting to change an established pattern of behaviour. Which of the statements below apply to your work with them?

☐ I provide frequent contact and support at the start.

☐ The empathy and rapport I gained with the service user is built on response to different needs.

☐ I help the service user divide goals into smaller steps.

☐ I ask questions such as, 'What will you achieve today/next week?'

☐ I help the service user visualise the success of each step, by asking for example, 'What will you see, hear think, feel when you reach your goal?'

☐ I help the service user identify visual reminders for achieving their goals, such as: a picture of the goal, a wall chart of the steps to take, photographs of them achieving each step.

☐ I help the service user celebrate success.

☐ I help the service user experience episodes of lapse as a learning experience.

☐ I ask, 'Who can help most?' and explore how they can be involved.

☐ I draw out self-motivating statements; helping the service user reframe, 'I can't' as 'I can', 'I'll try' as 'I will' and 'I failed' as 'I learn'.

☐ I help the service user identify and prepare for risky situations.

☐ I believe that the service user can change.

INTEGRATING ADDITIONAL SKILLS AND APPROACHES

Some changes will require a fundamental shift in lifestyle and behaviour. Someone who has abused alcohol or drugs from a young age may never have experienced adult life without the support of drugs. Someone who has learnt to believe that food will make them ugly, may never have learnt how to prepare, enjoy and eat food in a healthy way. In such circumstances, the cognitive behavioural techniques of modelling and teaching new behaviours and the provision of motivational feedback can be helpful. (Bandura 1965)

Being a Positive Role Model

Some of the people you work with may never have seen someone who demonstrates the behaviour they want to adopt. The novice skier for instance is likely to gain more by careful observation of a competent skier than from verbal guidance alone. By demonstrating the desired behaviour in your everyday interactions you can become a positive role model. Being a positive role model will require a focus on different behaviours according to the role you have.

- In the *health sector* a positive role model is likely to take particular care of their own health. Where patients are asked not to smoke, there is no sign of staff smoking; where patients are expected to eat healthily, staff eat healthily; where patients are expected to care for themselves, staff demonstrate personal care; where patients are expected to control their drinking or drug taking, staff control their own use of drugs.
- In the *criminal justice sector* a positive role model will demonstrate honesty, self-control, courtesy and reliability.
- In the *education sector* a positive role model will be willing to learn and explore ideas.
- In *social services* a positive role model will demonstrate self-responsibility, compassion for others and good problem-solving skills.
- In *youth* services a positive role model will demonstrate an ability to enjoy themselves responsibly, self-control and an ability to learn from mistakes.

In Chapter 3 we explored how learning is effective when all aspects of the Kolb cycle of learning are incorporated. Learning seems to be most effective when learners:

✓ Observe the desired behaviour in others

✓ Identify the key points from their observation

✓ Plan how to incorporate these into their own behaviour

✓ Practise the new behaviour

✓ Start the cycle again by reflecting on what went well and what could be done differently.

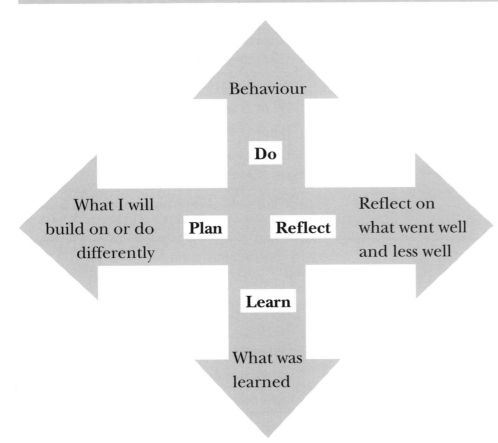

Source: Adapted from Kolb's (1984) learning cycle

Teaching by modelling integrates all aspects of Kolb's learning cycle and bridges the gap between a service user's understanding of what needs to be done and their skills to do it. The chart below is based on the stages of modelling identified by Brain Sheldon (1995) and shows how a motivational approach can support this cognitive behavioural intervention. The programme is useful at the action and maintenance stage. It can be undertaken either as one-to-one work, or as part of a group programme.

Learning from modelling (Service user's tasks)	Key motivational questions and summaries (Facilitator's tasks)
LEARN **Identify the problem and specific behaviour to change**	Recap of the problem and summarise a specific behaviour the service user has identified to change.
Divide behaviour into smallest possible parts	*What specifically is involved in a 'coping performance'?* *What is said in a 'coping performance'?* *What is the tone of voice like?* *What facial expressions are there?* *How do you stand, walk, etc.?* *What is the thinking behind each action?*
PLAN **Observe one way to complete the task** **Identify key steps**	*'One option would be for me to demonstrate a way of doing it and for you to then have a go. What do you think?'* *Provide a demonstration and invite the service user to break it down into key steps. Plan how to try them out*
DO **Practise a simplified performance in a safe setting**	Facilitator listens and observes behaviour, body language and tone of voice.

REFLECT Review performance	*What went well?* *What went less well?* Reflect what you saw and heard *'I also noticed...'*
LEARN Consider key learning points	*'What did you learn?'* Reflect and build on any self-motivating statements. Reframe as areas for learning any negative statements.
PLAN Plan for more complex situations, lapse and individual differences	*'Which situations do you find more difficult?'* *'What would you like me to include in a typical demonstration for you?'* *'Who else might you watch?'*
DO, REFLECT, LEARN, PLAN Gradually put into practice with reduced explicit reinforcement, reflect and draw out key learning points, plan for more self-responsibility and self-belief	Repeat the above stages for more complex situations. Support self-belief and self-responsibility to put it into practice with reduced support. *'When will you try it on your own?'* *'What makes you think you can do it?'*

MOTIVATIONAL FEEDBACK

Feedback on progress is an integral part of supporting change. Aim to provide feedback in a private and safe place at the first opportunity, while the experience is still fresh in the service user's mind.

Motivational feedback will again use the core motivational skills.

✓ **Affirm.** Focus on positives rather than negatives.

✓ **Listen** to the experience and views of the service user before expressing your observations and views.

✓ **Open questions.** Draw out comments and feedback from the service user related to the learning cycle.

✓ **Summarise** what you have seen and heard.

✓ **Support self-motivating statements** and the belief in change.

Motivational feedback is *jointly owned by the service user and the facilitator*, as opposed to more confrontational which is given only from the perspective of the critic.

Johari's Window (Luft 1970) provides a useful theoretical framework for motivational feedback.

Johari's Window

The window of those things known to self and known others (Might be how tall you are)	The window of those things known to others but not to self (Might be that you are seen as kind)
The window of those things known to self but not to others (Might be that you like spiders)	The window of those things not known to self and not known to others (Might be that you are dyslexic)

The box known to the novice skier, but not initially to their instructor might have been as follows.

Known to self and others	Known to others not to self
Known to self not to others I have a fear of losing control. I can't read instructions without reading glasses. My left foot hurts.	**Not known to self or others**

The motivational ski instructor will draw out as much of this information as possible prior to making their own assessment or providing feedback on behaviours. Without such knowledge giving feedback can be unproductive.

There may be aspects of the novice skier's behaviour which the novice is unaware of, but which the instructor can observe or hear. Few of us are aware of what specifically we do or our body language. The table below provides an example of what the instructor might have observed.

Known to self and others	Known to others not to self
	Emergency stop skills could be improved by facing downhill more. The right foot is operating better than the left foot.
Known to self not known to others	**Not known to self or others** Left boot is too tight.

There will be some aspects of behaviour, which remain unknown to all. In the case of our novice skier perhaps the left boot is too tight. This can only be discovered when both parties share their knowledge. You may be able to reveal more of this hidden information by using a video recording or when pertinent questions are asked, which spur self-exploration.

The aim of motivational work is to increase the window of knowledge that is apparent to the service user, in order to empower them to change

Known to self and others	Known to others not to self
I have a fear of losing control.	
I can't read instructions without reading glasses.	
My left foot hurts.	
My left boot is too tight.	
I need to face downhill more.	
I have seen and practiced an emergency stop.	
Known to self not known to others	**Not known to self or others**

Service User's Worksheet S15.1: Sharing Feedback

Record your own thoughts about change and obtain feedback from others.

Known to self and others	Known to others not to self
Known to self not to others	**Not known to self or others**

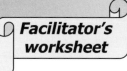

Facilitator's Worksheet F15.1: Providing Feedback

Reflect on a specific incident in which you provided feedback to a service user. Address the questions below as soon after the event as possible.

---

1. What was helpful about when and where feedback occurred?

How could I improve this for next time?

---

2. What worked well in gaining a self-assessment from the service user?

How could I improve this assessment?

---

3. How did I help the service user learn about their behaviour?

How could I have facilitated learning further?

---

4. To what extent did the service user want to, feel able to and ready to take up alternatives or repeat positive behaviour?

(Not ready) 0....1....2....3....4....5....6....7....8....9....10 (Ready)

What self-motivating statements did the service user make?

How did I help them to make them?

What else could I do next time?

Relapse or Recovery

The action and maintenance stage of change may be spread over weeks, months or longer. Lapse and going round the change cycle again and again are not uncommon during this time. Lapse is not failure; it is an opportunity to learn and to increase commitment. Most people who have successfully changed their lives have experienced periods of lapse.

SUMMARY

Patience and a return to the earlier stages of building desire and confidence are the way forward. The experience of the service user when they started to make a change can be used to strengthen conviction, confidence, and commitment throughout this process.

Where maintenance of the new behaviour is successful, many service users will rarely think about their previous behaviour. Others will always be aware of a significant change in their life, and how their improved life reinforces the changes they made.

A new lifestyle is built around the changed behaviour. They are content with the new behaviour and do not think of changing it. They have become 'pre-contemplational' about the new behaviour. They no longer need to tell themselves, 'I want to', 'I can', or 'I will change' instead they say, 'I have changed.'

> 'Success is the sum of small efforts, repeated day in day out.'
>
> *Robert Collier.*

Chapter 16

AN OVERVIEW OF THE MODEL

Chapters 3-15 describe the toolkit of skills and the strategies that are essential to a motivational approach. Knowing where to start motivational work with someone, and where to go next is pretty important. What you actually do is always a response to the particular circumstances of the unique individual you are working with. So you cannot proscribe a structure for motivational work that suits everyone. Nevertheless there is an overall strategy to the approach, set out in Chapter 1. You may find it useful to revisit Chapter 1 to get a new sense of the how skills work together to facilitate change.

The Facilitator worksheets, F6.3 and F6.4 in Chapter 6, based around the cycle of change, are a useful guide to the kinds of skills to use at each stage. The exercises suggested below also give an overview of work with an individual. Having a sense of the overall model will help the choices you make as a facilitator, as well as keep in mind what you are trying to achieve for the service user and your agency.

On the next page is a simplified reminder of the elements of the motivational approach (see Figure 16.1). Practice may be very different, moving between the stages in any order, and repeating some. The final part of this chapter is an overview of motivational work, portrayed as a dance.

Cultivating your motivational skills is a lifelong enterprise and this chapter suggests some of the tools you can employ. Firstly, you can explore peer coaching, in which you can rehearse the skills with colleagues. Secondly you can explore how managers and others in your organisation can help sustain a motivational approach.

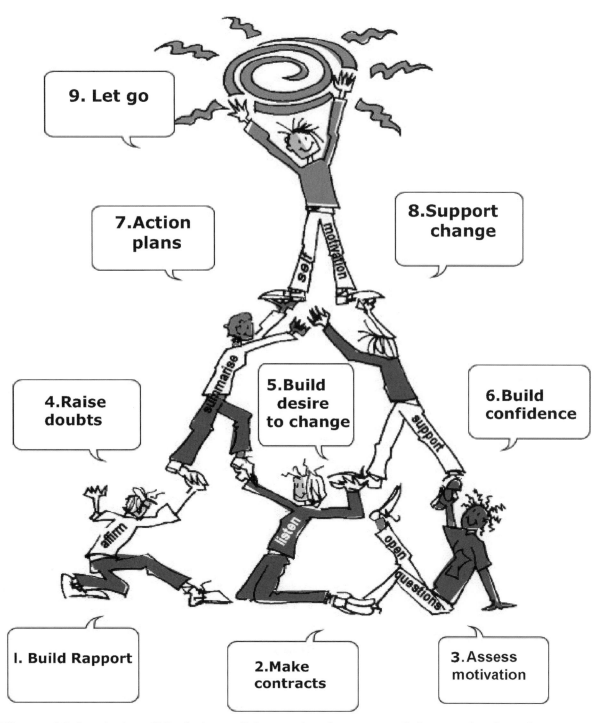

Figure 16.1 A simplified view of the main elements of the motivational approach. In practice you might move between the stages in any order, repeating some of them.

PEER COACHING

'Practice in a safe setting' means that you do not have to be perfect or even perform well to learn. You can learn from your mistakes and the mistakes of others, particularly when you are able to stop and try a different tack and observe a different outcome. Equally important you can notice what worked well and incorporate those skills into your practice.

Chapter 3 talked about the Kolb learning cycle, and how we learn by reflecting on experience. The Skills Coaching Cycle (Figure 16.2) was developed from Kolb's model by the authors and has been well tested in many training events. A facilitator's peer coaching exercise, using the model, is also described below.

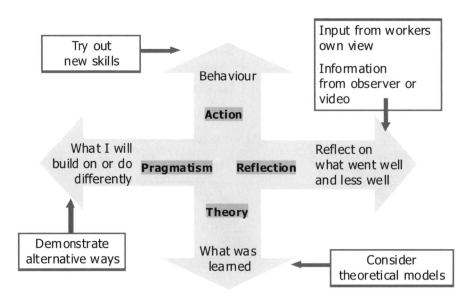

A Skills Coaching Cycle.
Source: P. Taylor and C. Fuller, 2004.

Similar learning opportunities can be established in supervision and team reviews. Wherever possible use real material from observation or videos. Learning from what worked well and what could be done differently is one of the most powerful ways of developing any skill. The exercises below are ideally rehearsed in small groups with colleagues who are also developing their motivational skills.

Facilitator's Worksheet F16.1: Peer Coaching, Suitable for Groups of 3-8 People

Resources required:

♦ Private, quiet room with no interruptions and plenty of space
♦ Chairs of equal size for each participant
♦ Video camera and tape, TV monitor for play back of video
♦ Observation guides (see below)
♦ Pens
♦ Examples of situations/scenarios for rehearsal (see F16.4 below), or ask participants to bring their own material.

Peer coaching

1. **Set up video camera** to focus on two chairs in the middle of the room. Other chairs are placed in a circle around them
2. **Appoint roles**
♦ Coach and facilitator for the session
♦ Interviewer
♦ Interviewee/service user
♦ Observer(s) if more than three participants.

The roles will be rotated after each coaching session.

3. **Work out the time slots** available to each participant for the interview and the feedback. Aim for 30-45 minutes per slot, 20 minutes is absolute minimum
4. **Provide all participants with an observation guide** to record evidence for the feedback sessions. (**See worksheets F16.2 and F16.3 below**)
5. **Decide an interview or interaction to rehearse.** Examples of possible situations are provided below. Some possible scenarios are suggested later in this chapter. You may wish to go through all the following stages or focus on those which can benefit from most rehearsal.

F16.1 continued...

a. Make contract

b. Building rapport

c. Raising doubt

d. Explore motivational balance

e. Building desire to change

f. Building confidence to change

g. Action planning

h. Supporting change

i. Let go

6. Put on the video camera and rehearse the interview

♦ The coach stops the interview preferably after a self-motivating statement has been made

7. The coach facilitates review and motivational feedback:

♦ The interviewer, then interviewee and then observers are asked to reflect:

'What went well?', 'What went less well?'

♦ The Feedback aims to describe specific behaviour and impact of that behaviour based on the observation sheet (see Chapter 15 for a discussion on effective feedback)

♦ The coach provides their own additional feedback and shows clips of the video

8. The interviewer is asked about learning and future development:

'What have you learnt?', 'What could you plan to do differently?'

Some participants benefit from the opportunity to try one or two bits again using a different approach and to see the different result.

Thank the interviewee and the interviewer for providing a learning opportunity for the rest of the group.

F16.1 continued...

Some learning points

Many participants say it is this session that helps them to see how all the skills fit together into a working tool.

Some participants may only be able to focus on some basic skills such as reflective listening. It is better to learn one thing well than skate over lots of skills. They can use the Toolkit to build their practice in the workplace. Others will find it comes naturally.

These are all learnable skills. Those with an apparent natural flair may have earlier experiences, which have taught them the skills. The less fluent participants simply need more opportunity for practise, observation and feedback.

It is crucial that each participant feels affirmed and positive about what each has learned. Even though some will have just made a start on the basic skills, others will be well on the way to competent practice.

It is important to have the video equipment set up and working beforehand. The practise time is precious and nothing is more frustrating than sorting out equipment faults instead of practising the skills.

The questions are only suggestions which can be added to or adapted to suit your needs.

Where time limits the possibility of all participants taking the role of the interviewer, ensure that everyone plays at least an interviewee. Much can be gained from this role. Some staff may not feel confident to be videoed. The motivational skills of drawing out the benefits of seeing themselves on video can be used. Check confidence on the 'I can' scale. If it is 5 or more they will probably want to see themselves on video.

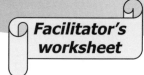

Facilitator's Worksheet F16.2: Observation Skills

Giving and receiving observation

Just one or two short points of feedback, supported by evidence from good observation is more useful than a long process recording. As with all motivational feedback it is offered in a matter of fact way to the person receiving it, as useful information from the observation, and never as criticism or a critique. To the receiver the information is a valued gift, from the observer.

A simple observation guide

The simple observation guide F16.3 below, is an aide-memoir to use when observing a piece of motivational work. Each observer can be given a copy for each person they observe. It helps the observer to break down the work into separate processes and skills and to note the effect of each component. The idea is to note down just a few short observations in detail. The observation guide can be used to record details of specific examples of language used, body language and tone of voice and the reaction it had. You will then have some useful evidence to give to the worker in the feedback session.

Further points for observation

◆ **Affirmation, valuing diversity**
   □ How far are the particular needs of this individual responded to?
   □ What positive things are said?
   □ How is the service user encouraged to feel positive about themselves?

◆ **Listening skills**
   □ Observe the body language as well as hearing the flow of conversation. What makes you think the interviewer is listening well?

F16.2 continued...

♦ **Open questions**

☐ Which questions were open and how much disclosure did they draw out?

☐ Which questions were particularly useful in helping the service user to think about their behaviour differently?

☐ Also note any closed questions. What was the response to the closed questions? How could you reframe these for the future?

♦ **Summarising and reflections**

☐ As you get more skilled in motivational work you will replace many open questions with reflections. What was the balance of questions and reflections?

☐ What was the impact of the reflections used?

☐ When would it have been helpful to reword a question as a reflection?

♦ **Self-motivating statements**

☐ What self-motivating statements were drawn out? e.g. *'This might be a problem.' 'My girlfriend is concerned about ...,' 'I am concerned about...,' 'It might be helpful to ...,' 'I want to change', 'I can do it', 'I will do it'.* How strong is the commitment language? To what extent does it increase or decrease during the interview.

♦ **Avoid argument/Build rapport**

☐ Listen out for any parts of the interview where the interview tries to persuade the service user to change and the response is, *'ah but'.* How could you respond differently?

☐ Observe body language, listen to tone of voice. What makes you think there is good rapport?

♦ **Motivational balance**

☐ How far are concerns with present behaviour and benefits of change explored?

☐ How far are the benefits of present behaviour and concerns about change listened to?

☐ How could this be developed further?

F16.2 continued...

♦ **Discrepancies identified**

   ☐ What discrepancies were identified between long-term goals and short-term behaviour?

♦ **Self-responsibility and self-belief**

   ☐ How far is the interviewee encouraged to consider what they can do to overcome difficulties? What questions and reflections help to build confidence?

Facilitator's Worksheet F16.3: Motivational Skills Observation Guide

	Skill	Examples from your observations
A	Affirming/valuing difference	
L	Listening	
O	Open Questions	
S	Summarises	
S	Support self-motivating statements	
	Arguments avoided/ Rapport built	
	Motivational balance explored	
	Discrepancies reflected	
	Self-responsibility and self-belief developed	

Facilitator's Worksheet F16.4:
Some Scenarios for Developing Skills,
for use in F16.1 above

(These suggestions can be adapted to your particular setting.)

Scenario One

Agenda setting and contracts

Purpose - to build rapport, to establish a joint agenda.

Situation

Jake has just arrived at your agency. He has difficulties with reading, writing and understanding complex language. Use motivational skills to build rapport and draw out his and the agency's expectations and responsibilities. Engage with Jake as much as possible by identifying and responding to particular needs, asking open questions and reflecting understanding.

You may not need to explore motivational balances or draw out discrepancies in this interview. You will need to know how far Jake has understood what the agency can offer, and what he is has been asked to do.

An ideal performance will include open questions, reflective listening and may include some information giving. Body language will be in harmony.

F16.4 continued...

Scenario Two

Assessing behaviour

Purpose - to establish rapport, to gain information, to establish a working relationship.

Situation

Saleem has just been referred to your agency for an assessment of need. He does not think he has a problem, others have referred him. Select an area of assessment you are likely to come across in your normal work situation. Incorporate motivational skills into a typical assessment. If there are standard closed questions you need to ask, decide how you can introduce these and open the assessment up afterwards.

An ideal performance will avoid argument, ah buts, direct confrontation (e.g. 'you have a drug problem') and collusion (avoiding the subject). Include open questions such as 'Tell me about ...' and summarise understanding.

F164 continued...

Scenario Three

Challenging racism without conflict

Purpose - to establish a joint agenda.

Situation

You have overheard Josh making racist jokes in front of a black service user. You have taken him aside to discuss this with him.

An ideal scenario will include gaining information, open questions and reflections.

Doubt will be raised without argument or direct confrontation.

F164 continued...

Scenario Four

Building desire to change

Purpose - to clarify concerns with present behaviour, develop desire to change.

Situation

Jake is starting to identify reasons, on the one hand, why he wants to develop his literacy skills (or select an area of change relevant to your work situation). On the other hand, he can think of several reasons to put the decision off. Help him to consider the reasons he would like to change and reasons for staying as he is.

An ideal performance will explore the motivational balance, will include listening, and open questions, drawing out self-motivating statements concerning the desire to change.

F164 continued...

Scenario Five

Overcoming obstacles

Purpose - to develop confidence

Situation

Maureen is due to attend a programme to address her drug taking (or select another intervention relevant to your work situation). She is expressing a number of reasons why she wants to attend the programme but also has some fears. Her desire to participate seems to be fairly high but her confidence low. Draw out what her fears are and what strengths and resources she has to overcome these. Use the confidence ladder (see worksheet S13.1) if helpful. Consider diversity issues and any barriers outside her sphere of influence. What options are available to help overcome the barriers? Identify those that she will consider. (see worksheets S13.1-S13.10)

An *ideal performance* will include listening, open questions, summarising and will draw out self-motivating statements of confidence and self-belief. You might also help her draw confidence from something she has done successfully in the past.

F16.4 continued...

Scenario Six

Motivational action planning

Purpose - to establish a workable action plan.

Situation

Continuation of scenario 5. Maureen has decided that she wants to stop taking drugs. Help her to identify an action plan, who will help and what the first steps will be. (Adapt to your own work situation.) Worksheets S14.1-S14.8 may be useful.

An *ideal performance* will explore desire and confidence to change prior to action planning. Commitment language will be drawn out. Options for the plan will be identified by the service user. The option chosen will be specific, measurable, achievable and relevant to the service user and time limited. A small first step will be identified for achieving the plan.

F16.4 continued...

Scenario Seven

Supporting change

Purpose - to develop new behaviours and skills.

Situation

Maureen has made her changes and moved to stay with an aunt and cousin who are both supportive in helping her to change. She has obtained supportive employment working part-time on a local farm. She has made some progress over the last four weeks. She is concerned that one of her previous friends has asked her to meet up and fears that she will be offered drugs. She has already said she will go, but would prefer not to. She is unsure how to say 'No', either to the meeting or once she meets her friend. Talk with her about the option of observing a demonstration and rehearsing the skills to say no. Refer to Chapter 15 for further guidance. (Adapt to your own work situation.)

An *ideal performance* will have listening, open questions, will summarise understanding, draw out statements of self-belief, break new behaviour down into small parts, give a clear demonstration and motivational feedback.

F16.4 continued...

Scenario Eight

Dispute between service users

Purpose - to develop self-responsibility

Situation

Nick grabs you in the corridor complaining about his room-mate who he says is dirty, smelly and noisy. He wants you to sort the situation out and give him a room to himself.

(Adapt to your work situation.)

An *ideal performance* will draw out self-motivating statements from Nick such as 'I want to...' 'I can...'

F164 continued...

Scenario Nine

Group work (For facilitators involved in delivering group work)

Purpose - to use motivational skills in a group setting

Situation

You are running a group work session. Craig arrives late, is very quiet, does not seem to understand what you are talking about and only provides one word answers. Other participants will play group participants. All of them will be involved. How can you use motivational skills in this setting?

An *ideal performance* will use simple language, open questions and reflections to check understanding. Some Socratic open questions might be tried (Chapter 12).

F164 continued...

Scenario Ten

Relapse

Purpose - to rebuild confidence and desire to change

Situation

Carol has attended four sessions of a weight maintenance programme. You've noticed that in the past week she looks more tired and pale. She says she can't be bothered to go to the programme this week as she doesn't need to. Use motivational skills to hear her concerns, develop discrepancy with longer-term goals and start to build confidence.

(Adapt to your own work situation.)

An *ideal performance* will include identifying strengths, listening, reflecting and affirming. What were the benefits of change? What worked well in the past?

F164 continued...

Scenario Eleven

Community reintegration: Letting go

Purpose - To develop the service user's own networks and resources for continued change.

Situation

Maureen has been controlling a drug habit for the last 18 months. There have been occasional lapses but steady progress has been made. Help her to identify how she will continue to maintain the behaviour without your agency involvement.

An *ideal performance* will including, listening, affirming progress, drawing out self-motivating statements of confidence, discussing who will help and how to overcome potential risky situations.

ADDITIONAL TOOLS FOR DEVELOPING MOTIVATIONAL SKILLS

- **Read**
  - ◆ See References section at the end of this book
  - ◆ Browse this Toolkit

- **Take notice**
  - ◆ Of what you are doing
  - ◆ Of the response of the people you are working with

- **Mull over**
  - ◆ What has happened
  - ◆ What worked and what you could do differently

- **Try out**
  - ◆ Different approaches and note the results
  - ◆ In this way increase your repertoire of responses

- **Learn from others**
  - ◆ Each individual is unique and we will learn from each one

- **Receive feedback**
  - ◆ From service users - how did they experience your work
  - ◆ From the observation of colleagues
  - ◆ Using the observation guides
  - ◆ From videos of your work
  - ◆ From managers about the outcome of our work

- **Give feedback to others**
  - ◆ The act of observing and giving considered feedback increases the learning of the feedback giver as well as the receiver

THE MANAGER'S ROLE IN SUSTAINING AND DEVELOPING MOTIVATIONAL SKILLS
Motivational managers

Use the skills in their own practice.

Model the skills to staff.

Establish structures to support and affirm motivational skills.

Know how to develop motivational skills for the role of the team.

Motivational skills are also essential skills for managers. Motivating, affirming and developing staff is crucial to service delivery. The motivational approach also works well when listening to the concerns of staff, clarifying issues or dealing with conflict.

Successful managers do not always need to have the skills of those they manage, but with motivational skills they are in a position to model the skills as well as use them to enable staff.

STRUCTURES TO SUPPORT MOTIVATIONAL SKILLS

If motivational skills are seen as entirely the responsibility of practitioners or a quick fix to increase successful outcomes, they are unlikely to be effective. The motivational approach needs to be authorised and resourced in such a way that they are integral to the policies, structures, procedures, professional methods and training plans of the organisation.

Outcomes

Within a team it is helpful if there is a clear, shared, understanding of when motivational approaches are likely to be effective, and how these contribute to the outcomes required of the team. This will probably require work at team meetings, especially where motivational skills are new to some members and some roles.

To nurture and develop motivational skills, consider the following:

- ◆ Supervision based on evidence using the guides in Chapter 11

- ◆ Team review days.

- ◆ Paired working with an agreement for observation and feedback

- ◆ Basic training days

- ◆ Specialist training days

- ◆ Using the toolkit individually or in small groups.

Team Review Days

One possible model for a team review day is:

Session 1	Recap of a chapter from the Toolkit.
Session 2	Using video or observation reports, review actual pieces of work undertaken by team members, look at what worked well and what might be done differently.
Session 3	Discussion of the implications and learning.
Session 4	Make a team action plan.

Priorities

The amount of time that a team or an individual can devote to developing motivational skills will depend on the importance of those skills in meeting the outcomes required of the team. If the skills become part of the team culture, they become self-sustaining.

Facilitator's worksheet

Facilitator's Worksheet F16.5: Exercise – Where next?

1. Word storm the situations where you will use motivational skills in your specialist role

2. What are the benefits of using motivational skills

   The benefits for me are...

   The benefits for the team/agency are...

   The benefits for the service user are..

3. What are the barriers to using the skills?

4. How will you overcome these barriers?

5. Who else can help?

F16.5 continued...

6. What are options for your next steps?

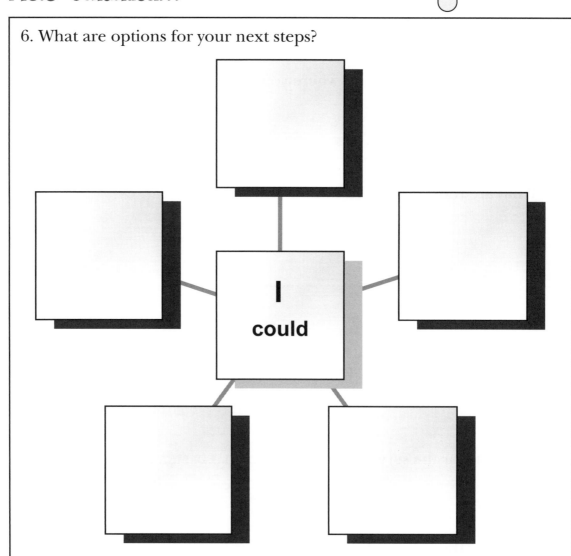

I could

7. Which option will you select for your next step? (Consider the advantages and disadvantages of a couple of options if helpful.)

8. What specifically will you do by when?

By.................. I will

....

9. How confident are you that you will do this?

0   1   2   3   4   5   6   7   8   9   10

TOWARDS A MOTIVATIONAL CULTURE

Motivational skills are relevant to every role in the organisation from reception to the director general. A motivational approach improves communication, teamwork and the sense of purpose of the whole organisation. It is not just for use with service users. Not everybody in the organisation needs to be an expert in motivational interviewing. Many of the skills can be incorporated in everyday activities from giving and receiving information to handling misunderstandings. As you use this Toolkit you may find at first you become conscious of your communication style. As you build the skills the motivational spirit will become part of your everyday practice. Interactions that were once a battle become a dance.

THE MOTIVATIONAL DANCE

The Motivational Dance

Take your partner and form up where they are now (Spot the position on the cycle of change)

Match and reflect to build empathy

Go through all the steps for staying the same or changing (the motivational balance)

Explore long term goals

Lead them towards contemplation of change by developing discrepancy

If they change the dance, change with them, don't tread on their toes

They may reach a point of decision, and dance away from it again

Repeat the steps of exploring, staying the same or changing, whenever ambivalence undermines decision

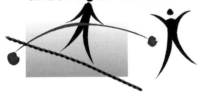

Decision to Action - Help them over the hurdles

Lapse is only a step in the dance

Encourage them to take the lead and build the confidence to do it for themselves

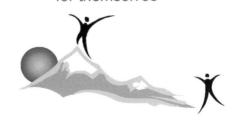

REFERENCES

Amrhein, P., Miller, W., Yahne, C., Palmer, M. and Fulcher, L. (2003) Client commitment language during motivational interviewing predicts drug use outcomes. *Journal of Consulting and Clinical Psychology,* 71, 862–878.

Bailey, A. and Egan, G. (1999) *Talk Works 2, How to get more out of life through better conversations.* London: British Telecom.

Bandura, A. (1965) Influence of models reinforcement contingencies on the acquisition of imitative responses. *Journal of Personality and Social Psychology,* 1, 589–595.

Bandura, A. (1977) *Social Learning Theory.* Englewood Cliffs, NJ: Prentice-Hall.

Barrowclough, C., Haddock, G., Tarrier, N., Lewis, S.W., Moring, J., O'Brien, R., Schofield, N. and McGovern, J. (2001) Randomized controlled trial of motivational interviewing, cognitive behaviour therapy, and family intervention for patients with combined schizophrenia and substance use disorders. *American Journal of Psychiatry,* 158, 1706–1713.

Belcher, L., Kalichma, S., Topping, M., Smith, S., Emshoff, J., Norris, F. and Nurss, J. (1998) A randomised trial of a brief HIV risk reduction counselling intervention for women. *Journal of Consulting and Clinical Psychology,* 66, 856–861.

Deci, E.L. and Ryan, R.M. (1985) *Intrinsic Motivation and Self-determination on Human Behaviour.* New York: Plenum Press.

DiClemente, C.C. (2006) *Addiction and Change.* New York: Guildford Press.

Dilorio, C., Resnicow, K., McDonnell, M., Soet, J., McCarty, F. and Yeager, K. (2003) Using motivational interviewing to promote adherence to antiretroviral medications: A pilot study. *Journal of the Association of Nurses in AIDS care,* 14(2), 52–62.

Dowden, C. and Andrews, D.A. (2004). The importance of staff characteristics in delivering effective correctional treatment: A meta-analytic review of core correctional practice. *International Journal of Offender Therapy and Comparative Criminology,* 48, 203–215.

Festinger, L. (1957) *A Theory of Cognitive Dissonance.* Evanston, IL: Row Peterson.

Gershoff, E.T. (2002) Corporate punishment by parents and associated child behaviours and experiences: A meta-analysis and theoretical review. *Psychological Bulletin,* 128, 539–579.

Gordon, T. (1970) *Parent Effectiveness Training.* New York, Wyden.

Harris, K.B. & Miller, W.R (1990) Behavioural self-control training for problem drinkers: Components of efficacy. *Psychology of Addictive Behaviours,* 4, 82–90.

Harper, R. and Hardy, S. (2000) An evaluation of motivational interviewing as a method of intervention with clients in a probation setting. *British Journal of Social Work,* 30, 393–400.

Heather, N., Rollnick, S., Bell, A. and Richmond, R. (1996) Effects of brief counselling among male heavy drinkers identified on general hospital wards. *DrugTherapy,* 23, 325–334.

Hettema, J.E., Miller, W.R. and Steele, J.M. (2004) A meta-analysis of motivational interviewing techniques in the treatment of alcohol use disorders. *Alcoholism-Clinical and Experimental Research,* 28, 74A.

Hodgins, D.C., Currie, S.R. and el-Guebaly, N. (2001). Motivational enhancement and self-help treatments for problem gambling. *Journal of Consulting and Clinical Psychology,* 69, 50–57.

Honey, P. & Mumford, A. (1986) *Using your Learning Style.* Maidenhead: Honey Publications.

Janis, I.L. and Mann, L. (1977) *Decision-making: A psychological analysis of conflict, choice and commitment.* New York: Free Press.

Kear-Colwell, J. and Pollock, P. (1997) Motivation or confrontation: which approach to child sex offender? *Criminal Justice and Behaviour,* 24, 20–33.

Kemp, R., Kirov, G., Everitt, B., Hayward, P. and David, A. (1998) Randomised controlled trial of compliance theory: 18 month follow-up. *British Journal of Psychiatry,* 172, 413–419.

Kohn, A. (2000) *Punished by Rewards: The Trouble with Gold Stars, Incentive Plans, A's, Praise and Other Bribes.* New York: Houghton Mifflin.

Kolb, D. (1984) *Experiential Learning.* Englewood Cliffs, NJ: Prentice Hall.

Laborde, G.L. (1987) *Influencing and Integrity.* Syntony Publishing, Palo Alto, CA.

Leake, G.J. and King, A.S. (1977) Effect of counsellor expectation on alcoholic recovery. *Alcohol, Health and Research Work,* 11, 16–22.

Lipsey, M.W. (1992) Juvenile delinquency treatment; A meta- analytic inquiry into the variability of effects. In T.Cook, H.Cooper, D.S. Cordray, H. Hartmann, L.V. Hedges, R.J. Light, T.A. Louise and F. Mostellerl (Eds) *Meta-analysis for Explanation: A Casebook.* New York: Russell Sage Foundation.

Luborsky, L., McLellan, A.T., Woody, G.E., O'Brien, C.P. and Auerbach, A. (1985). Therapist success and its determinants. *Archives of General Psychiatry, 42,* 602–611.

Luft, J. (1970) *Group Process,* 2nd edn. Palo Alto, CA: Press Books.

Mann, R.E. and Rollnick, S. (1996) Motivational interviewing with a sex offender who believed he was innocent. *Behavioural and Cognitive Psychotherapy, 24,* 127–134.

Mehrabian, A. (1972) *Non verbal Communication* Chicago, IL: Aldine Atherstone.

Mckee, D. (1980) *Not now Bernard.* London: Red Fox.

Miller, W.R. (Ed.) (1980) *The Addictive Behaviours: Treatment of Alcoholism, Drug Abuse, Smoking, and Obesity.* New York: Pergamon Press.

Miller, W.R. and Rollnick, S. (1991) *Motivational Interviewing – Preparing People to Change Addictive Behaviour.* New York: Guildford Press.

Miller, W.R. and Rollnick, S. (2002) *Motivational Interviewing – Preparing People to Change* (2nd edn). New York: Guildford Press.

Miller, W.R., Benefield, R.G. and Tonigan, J.S. (1993) Enhancing motivation for change in problem drinking: A controlled comparison of two therapist styles. *Journal of Consulting and Clinical Psychology, 61,* 455–461.

Miller, W.R., Yahne, C.E. and Tonigan, J.S. (2003). Motivational interviewing in drug abuse services: A randomized trial. *Journal of Consulting and Clinical Psychology,* 71(4), 754–763.

Monti, P.M. et al (1999) Brief intervention for harm reduction with alcohol-positive older adolescents in a hospital emergency department. *Journal of Consulting and Clinical Psychology,* 67(6), 989–994.

Pascal, B. (1960) *Oeuvres Complètes.* Paris: Seuil.

Prochaska, J. and Di Clemente, C.C. (1982) Trans-theoretical therapy; towards a more integrative model of change. *Psychotherapy; Theory, Research and Practice, 19,* 276–288.

Project MATCH Research Group (1997) Project MATCH secondary a priori hypotheses. *Addiction, 92,* 1671–1698.

Resnicow, K., Dilorio, C., Soet, J., Borelli, B., Hecht, J. and Ernst D. (2002) Motivational interviewing in health promotion: it sounds like something is changing. *Health Psychology,* 21(5), 444–451.

Roberts, C. (2003) The emerging what works evidence and its implications for practice in the National Probation Service, *National Probation Service What Works Conference 2003 pack. A whole service approach to delivering intervention* 8–10 December, Nottingham.

Rogers, C.R. (1951) *Client Centered Therapy,* Boston, MA: Houghton-Mifflin.

Rollnick, S. (2003) Motivational interviewing, *National Probation Service What Works Conference Pack. A whole service approach to delivering intervention,* 8–10 December, Nottingham.

Rosenthal, R. and Jacobson, L. (1992) *Pygmalion in the Classroom: Teacher expectation and pupils' intellectual development.* New York: Irvington.

Sellman, J.D., Sullivan, P.F., Dore, G.M., Adamson, S.J. and MacEyouan, I. (2001) A randomized controlled trial of motivational enhancement therapy (MET) for mild to moderate alcohol dependence. *Journal of Studies on Alcohol,* 62, 389–396.

Sheldon, B. (1995) *Cognitive Behavioural Therapy.* London: Routledge.

Tannen, D. (1992) *You Just don't Understand: Men and women in conversation.* London: Virago.

Treasure, J. and Ward, A. (1997) A practical guide to the use of motivational interviewing in anorexia nervosa. *European Eating Disorders Review,* 5, 102–114.

Trotter, C. (1999) *Working with Involuntary Clients: A guide to practice.* London: Sage.

West, C. (1990) Not just 'doctors' orders': directive-response sequences in patients' visits to women and men physicians. *Discourse and Society,* 1(1), 85–112.

Woollard, J., Beilin, L., Lord, T., Puddey, I., MacAdam, D. and Rouse, I. (1995) A control trial of nurse counselling on lifestyle change for hypertensives treated in general practice: preliminary results. *Clinical and Experimental Pharmacology and Physiology,* 22(6–7), 466–468.

Facilitator Worksheets

F15.4	Observation skills	16	264–266
F15.5	Motivational skills observation guide	16	267
F15.6	11 Scenarios for developing skills	16	268–278
F15.7	Where next	16	283–284

Service User's Worksheets

Worksheet Number	Service User's Worksheet Title	Chapter	Page
S5.1	Exploring current motivation	5	69
S6.1	Self assessment of motivation to change	6	78
S6.2	Where am I on the cycle of change	6	82
S6.3	Alternative cycle of change	6	83
S6.4	Exploring change-thoughts, feelings and behaviour	5	84
S11.1	Motivational Balance	11	179
S11.2	Exploring ambivalence step 1 - My life in a year's time	11	181
S11.3	Exploring ambivalence step 2 - I want to	11	182
S11.4	Exploring ambivalence step 3 - motivational balance	11	183
S12.1	Who I am and Who I want to become	12	202
S12.1	What do I want to change	12	203
S12.3	Source of motivation	12	204
S12.4	I want to	12	205
S13.1	I can-step 1	13	211
S13.2	I can-step 2	13	212
S13.3	I can-step 3	13	213
S13.4	I can-step 4	13	215
S13.5	I can-step 5	13	216
S13.6	I can-step 6	13	217
S13.7	I can-step 7	13	218
S13.8	I can-step 8	13	219
S13.9	I can-step 9	13	220
S13.10	I can-step 10	13	221
S14.1	Clarifying outcomes	14	234
S14.2	Belief in change	14	235
S14.3	Negotiating a plan-options	14	237
S14.4	Shall I do this or that?	14	239
S14.5	First steps	14	241
S14.6	Putting it into practice	14	242
S15.1	Sharing feedback	15	255